CHARTING A NEW COURSE

Mike Mansfield and
U.S. Asian Policy

CHARTING
A NEW COURSE

Mike Mansfield and
U.S. Asian Policy

Four Reports by
Mike Mansfield, Senator

with a brief biography by
William D. James

CHARLES E. TUTTLE COMPANY
Rutland, Vermont & Tokyo, Japan

Representatives

Continental Europe: BOXERBOOKS, INC., *Zurich*

British Isles: PRENTICE-HALL INTERNATIONAL, INC., *London*

Canada: HURTIG PUBLISHERS, *Edmonton*

Australasia: BOOK WISE (AUSTRALIA) PTY. LTD.
104–108 Sussex Street, Sydney 2000

*Published by the Charles E. Tuttle Company, Inc.
of Rutland, Vermont & Tokyo, Japan
with editorial offices at
Suido 1-chome, 2-6, Bunkyo-ku, Tokyo, Japan*

Library of Congress Catalog Card No. 77-83044

International Standard Book No. 0-8048-1257-8

First edition, 1978

PRINTED IN JAPAN

TABLE OF CONTENTS

53450

PUBLISHER'S FOREWORD

The selection of Mike Mansfield as American ambassador to Japan has been greeted with open enthusiasm by the government, press, and people of Japan. Part of the reason for this is, of course, that the ambassador is known to be a man of high principles, consideration, and open mind. He would be a welcome representative in any country. More important, though, is that the selection of Mr. Mansfield, an acknowledged expert on Asian affairs, implies the long-awaited recognition by the American government of Japan as, to quote the ambassador himself, "a factor to be reckoned with in its capacity to influence the flow of international events."

Our position as one of the oldest and largest English-language publishers in Japan has enabled us to watch closely Japan's growth in thirty years from a war-ravaged, disheartened country to the world's second-ranking industrial democracy. We like to think that our efforts to produce informative books on Japanese culture have helped minimize friction between Japan and other nations during this remarkably productive period. It was with a sense of our role in Japan that we, upon hearing of Mr. Mansfield's appointment, began to search for a means of providing both Japanese and Americans with a glimpse of the new ambassador and some indication of the policies he would likely pursue during his tenure.

We are pleased to reprint in full the reports made by Senator Mansfield so that they may have wider circulation among the general public. We hope, too, that the comprehensive subject index specially prepared for this book will facilitate free and rapid dialogues between Japanese and American leaders, analysts, journalists, and students. The recent change of administrations in the United States, the attainment by Japan of a significant position among world leaders, and the problems yet unsolved in Asia demand that the peoples of Japan and America perceive each other not with illusions but with their eyes open to the real challenges that await them. This book has been prepared with that need in mind.

MIKE MANSFIELD: A Portrait

In 1917 a fourteen-year-old grade-school student in Great Falls, Montana, named Mike Mansfield confided to his sisters that he wanted to join the Navy and see the world.

He accomplished both goals. The slender, round-faced boy ran away from home, joined the Navy before he was fifteen by fibbing about his age, crossed the Atlantic Ocean seven times on the U.S.S. *Minneapolis,* and had glimpses of Europe that whetted his interest in travel. The *Minneapolis,* a cruiser from the Spanish-American War, was on convoy duty in the Atlantic during World War I.

Mansfield was discharged from the Navy in August, 1919, and worked briefly on a ranch in Montana. He then joined the Army, hoping to be assigned to occupation duty in Germany. Instead, his commanding officer at Fort McDowell near San Francisco, thinking the Montanan must know something about horses, assigned him to care for the horses and to teach officers' children how to ride.

Mansfield was sorely disappointed that his Army service didn't give him the opportunity to travel that his Navy term had. As a sailor, he had visited Britain, France, and the Azores. Wanting to get in more traveling, he enlisted for a two-year term in the Marines as soon as he was discharged from the Army.

"I really hit the jackpot then," said Mansfield. And no wonder, for his Marine experience took him to the Far East and stimulated a lifelong interest in Far Eastern history.

Mansfield's marine battalion was stationed on "Russian Island" off the Siberian coast at a time when American and allied troops were trying to influence the outcome of the Russian Civil War. He also served with troops on patrol and guard duty on the outskirts of Tientsin, China. Mansfield was discharged from the Marines on November 6, 1922—at age nineteen a veteran of the Navy, Army, and Marines, and Montana's youngest World War I veteran.

But when Mansfield was a boy, swimming or playing run-sheep-run, he probably never dreamed about the numerous trips he would take later—many at the request of eight United States presidents. The young Mansfield might also have questioned the sanity of anyone predicting in 1917 that he would become one of the most influential persons in government and chalk up an enviable record that would win him national and international respect.

The boy from Great Falls rose higher in the United States government than any other Montanan ever has, but when he retired from the Senate he did so in the low-key, modest manner that has marked his entire career. He was the first retiring senator to clear his offices to make way for his successor (present Senate Majority Leader Robert Byrd of Virginia), and in the weeks leading up to his retirement, Mansfield continued to treat his colleagues with great consideration. Commenting on his retirement plans, announced in March of 1976, Mansfield explained that neither his age (73) nor health was responsible. Characteristically, he said that it was just time to step down.

"I just thought it was time for somebody else to shoulder the burden and the responsbility," he told the press.

Mansfield served five two-year terms in the House of Representatives before going to the Senate in 1953. Only after considerable persuasion from then Senate Majority Leader Lyndon B. Johnson did Mansfield accept the post of Assistant Majority Leader (Whip), which he held for four years. Then, following a personal plea from Pres. John F. Kennedy, Mansfield became Senate Majority Leader, a post he held for a record sixteen years.

Mansfield's base of influence in the Senate included the chairmanship of the Senate Steering Committee, which assigns Democratic senators to committees, and the Senate Democratic Conference, which includes all Democratic senators. Mansfield, the tenth-ranking senator in seniority when he retired, was the second-ranking member on the influential Senate Foreign Relations Committee and chairman of its Far Eastern Subcommittee. He was a key member of the powerful Senate Appropriations Committee and chairman of the Military Construction Subcommittee of the Senate Armed Forces Committee.

A quiet, gentle man, he has worn his power and influence as gracefully as he does the 175 pounds on his slender six-foot frame. His open, weathered face, often described as Lincolnesque, breaks into a pleasant smile when he discusses his "power."

"The Majority Leader has very little power," Mansfield told Julius Duscha for an article in *Washingtonian Magazine*. "And what authority you have is on sufferance from your colleagues. I operate on the basis that I treat my colleagues, regardless of seniority or political differences, the way I would like to be treated. I don't desire power as such. I'd like to get away from it. I like to get by on cooperation, understanding, and mutual trust. I have no desire to be in a position where I can crack a whip. I don't want to tell people what to do. Senators are mature. They can arrive at a judgment."

Mansfield explained that he sometimes would tell a senator: "If you're in doubt, give your leader the benefit of the doubt." But he added, "I have rarely specifically asked a man to vote a certain way."

The change in the Majority Leader's office when Mansfield assumed it was dramatic. Lyndon B. Johnson, said to have been the most powerful leader in history, browbeat senators, threatened them, coaxed and cajoled them, tugged at their coat lapels, and kneaded their elbows. Sometimes Johnson worked the senators over so roughly, that, as he put it, "the skin comes off with the fur."

Johnson grasped all the ganglia of Senate power and he never let them go.

Senators chuckled when the mild-mannered Mansfield succeeded Johnson. "It's going to be a new show," one senator commented.

"Mansfield and Johnson are about as similar as Winston Churchill and St. Francis of Assisi," said another. When Mansfield became the leader, each senator was said to have grown an inch overnight and to have blossomed like a flower.

Mansfield didn't believe in a one-man or boss-dominated Senate, and he set out immediately to disperse responsibility. He treated each senator, from the newest to the most senior, with respect and consideration. When criticized for not being a more powerful leader in the Johnson tradition, Mansfield said he was neither a circus ringmaster nor a wheeler and dealer.

He is proud that through an evolutionary process the Senate has changed greatly and become a more responsible and democratic body. He finds it amusing that the changes in the Senate have been effected so quietly that they have received little publicity or national attention. But he has frequently said the Senate under his leadership has a record of accomplishment that will compare favorably with that of the Senate in any other period.

Mansfield's tact, consideration, and decency, and his policy of following the golden rule have been credited with gaining him the confidence, trust, and love of Republicans and Democrats alike. His Senate colleagues, in fact, have voted him that body's most popular member. In 1964, Senate Minority Leader Everett Dirksen of Illinois, a close, personal friend of Mansfield, was asked by Republicans to take an effective role in the campaign.

"I'd go to the moon to help Republicans, but please don't ask me to go to Montana," Dirksen said.

Mansfield was the victim of a political smear in the 1970 campaign, with charges that he was "soft on communism" and implications that he was a national-security risk. Top Republicans in the Senate rallied to his defense, among them Sen. John J. Williams of Delaware, often called the conscience of the Senate.

"I have never met a more loyal or dedicated public servant than Mike Mansfield. I have the highest regard for him, his patriotism, his integrity, loyalty, and as a great American . . . there is no man I respect more," said Williams in reply to the charges.

In 1964 a close journalist friend of President Johnson wrote that Johnson was considering Mansfield as his running mate that year. Mansfield went immediately to the White House and told the president that under no conditions would he accept the vice-presidential role. Mansfield was mentioned on several occasions as a possibility for president or vice-president, but he rebuffed all such speculation, saying he had achieved his highest ambition when he became senator from Montana.

Pres. Gerald Ford, praising Mansfield when he set a new record for length of time as Senate Majority Leader, said Mansfield was a perfect example that nice guys don't have to finish last. Bullies, said Ford, don't always win.

And if more testimony to Mansfield's character is needed, one could point to the congratulatory messages he received upon his retirement. They would fill many scrapbooks. They came from President Ford, then President-elect Jimmy Carter, heads of many foreign governments, and almost all the important government and political leaders in the nation.

As Mansfield neared the end of his distinguished senatorial career, he frequently was asked what he considered his greatest achievements.

First of all, he has said, was the way he was able to use his congressional offices to help unsnarl the federal bureaucracy for thousands of fellow Montanans with countless problems involving such things as passports, Social Security, and the Veteran's Administration. He is proud, too, of the contributions he has made to the quality of life in Montana and to the state's facilities—its hospitals and schools.

"That's what my fellow Montanans sent me to Washington for. They sent me to represent them and I tried to do my best," he says modestly.

Although he never neglected his responsiblities as Majority Leader, Mansfield made a distinct point of seeing that the interests of his state always came first. He was known to have kept Cabinet officials cooling their heels in an outer office while greeting unexpected visitors from Montana.

Mansfield is proud, too, of his role in getting adopted the Twenty-sixth Amendment to the Constitution, which gave the right to vote to eighteen-year-olds. The Senate approved his resolution 94 to 0 on March 10, 1971, and the House passed it later by a 401 to 19 vote. The amendment became effective in July of 1971 when the thirty-ninth state approved it.

But he is especially proud that he initiated the Senate investigation into the Watergate affair and was responsible for getting Sen. Sam Ervin to head the special Senate committee. He has worked against political espionage and massive spending in elections, which he has said present a serious threat to the nation's form of government, and points with satisfaction to the important part he played in instigating congressional investigations into the excesses of the FBI and CIA.

Historians and Senate colleagues give Mansfield high marks for his insight and knowledge about Southeast Asian problems. His knowledge of the Far East has been recognized by every president from Franklin D. Roosevelt through Pres. Jimmy Carter, and President Carter's appointment of Mansfield as ambassador to Japan is only the most recent example of the role Mansfield has played in United States foreign policy. Presidents Roosevelt, Truman, Eisenhower, Kennedy, Johnson, Nixon, and Ford all asked Mansfield to head missions to study overseas problems, particularly those in the Far East.

His scholarly reports, dating back to the early 1950s, warned about becoming entangled in Southeast Asian wars. Mansfield showed his opposition to the growing American role in the Vietnam War in his usual quiet manner. He never made a trip to the White House during the Johnson and Nixon administrations without an updated report on the number of Americans killed and wounded. He gave the presidents the casualty reports.

Asked what he thought about during his frequent breakfast meetings in the White House with President Nixon, when their views were so far apart on the war and many other issues, he replied quickly:

"If I can shorten this war by even one day, I'll go anytime I'm asked." He indicated he would also go anyplace and meet anyone if that would help end the tragic war.

Known as a person with a deep reverence for the presidency, Mansfield said all American should look upon that office with respect. His reverence, however, didn't stop him from living up to his obligation to speak his mind when he thought it necessary—and Presidents Johnson and Nixon knew the gentle man from Montana would stick by his principles even if a president were trying to change his mind.

When announcing his retirement, Mansfield said he had an obligation to spend more time with his wife, Maureen, to whom he has always given the credit for whatever success he has attained. It was Maureen, then Maureen Hayes, a comely, copper-haired English teacher at Butte (Montana) High School, who encouraged him to get a formal education.

When Mike first met Maureen (her sister introduced them), he was working in the Butte mines as a mucker (shoveler) of ore. She had a degree from St. Mary's College in Indiana, and he, having run away to join the Navy, had less than an eighth-grade education.

Shortly after they met, he enrolled in a correspondence course. Then, while working in the Butte mines, he took a special examination to gain entry to the Montana School of Mines (now Montana Tech). Mansfield never forgot the break the Butte college gave him, and he has shown his appreciation in countless ways. When Montana Tech was threatened with being downgraded as a state university unit, he pulled strings in Washington and got the highly promising Magneto Hydrodynamics research facility for Butte.

Encouraged by Maureen Hayes to study, Mansfield left his job in the Butte mines in 1928 to enroll at the University of Montana at Missoula. He worked at two jobs while he studied for both his college degree and his Butte High School diploma.

In 1932 Maureen quit her teaching job in Butte to join Mansfield, her fiancé. They were married that autumn and both attended classes at the university.

Times were tough for the young couple in that depression period. Once when they were short of enough money to pay the rent for their quarters, Maureen cashed in her insurance policy. When Mansfield protested indignantly, she replied, "Be sensible, Mike—keeping you in school is our insurance for the future."

While working for his university degree, Mansfield managed to complete his high school studies, thus becoming a regularly enrolled university student during the last quarter of his senior year.

But even with a high school diploma and a college degree, the job market was discouraging in 1933. The chairman of the university history department offered Mansfield a graduate assistantship teaching two history courses for twenty-five dollars a month. He also worked part-time in the registrar's office. Mansfield's master's thesis, "United States–Korean Diplomatic Relations: 1866–1910," was completed during 1934.

Mansfield taught classes in Far Eastern and Latin American history and also lectured some years on Greek and Roman history. He was a popular instructor and made friends with his students, who turned out to be a valuable source of support when he entered politics.

When defeated in his first try at electioneering—for western district congressman in 1940—Mansfield didn't give up. He decided to win the next election and he did—the race for Congress in 1942. He went on to win four successive elections for the House before he won his first Senate term in 1952. The 1940 election was the only one he ever lost.

Mike Mansfield was born in New York City on March 16, 1903, the first son of Patrick J. Mansfield and Josephine O'Brien Mansfield, both emigrants from Ireland.

His mother died in 1910 and his father, not knowing how to take care of three young children, asked his uncle, Richard Mansfield, and his wife, Margaret, to help. The three small children came to live in the back rooms of a small grocery store in Great Falls, Montana. Mike lived there for seven years.

Richard Mansfield died in 1912, and Aunt Margaret took over the operation of the store—with help from Mike and his sisters, who remember him as a serious boy who liked to read and to sit and think. They recall he had a pet rabbit and tried violin lessons—which didn't take. Mike and his pals swam in the bay, shot marbles, played run-sheep-run and baseball, and they earned extra pocket money shoveling snow, delivering newspapers, and cutting grass. Mike was a familiar sight around town, pushing a cart loaded with groceries from his aunt's store. At first it had been a horse-drawn wagon, but, Mansfield now jokes, when the horse died he had to push the grocery cart by hand, thus entitling him to his first pair of shoes.

Doubtless the boy daydreamed about his future, little realizing how bright it was to be. How amused he would have been if someone had predicted then that his aunt's small home would be visited by two United States presidents. Lyndon B. Johnson visited there in 1960, when he was a candidate for vice-president, and Pres. John Kennedy stopped by in September of 1963, making a hit the Irish Mansfields will never forget.

But Mike was restless and craved to get out and see something of the world. He ran away from home twice. Once he had to spend a night in the local jail. The third time he ran away he made it. From June of 1917 to February of 1918, he traveled, riding the rails in railroad freight cars. He is proud that he never had to beg for food.

"I never had to bum food once," he said in an interview. He worked in lumber camps to earn money for his meals.

In February of 1918, he appeared at the New York City home of his father, who had remarried by then. The fourteen-year-old boy asked permission to join the Navy and tried to persuade his father to sign a paper saying he was seventeen. When his father declined to do so, Mansfield resorted to a white lie and talked the Navy recruiters into letting him enlist.

Mike Mansfield is now the twenty-second American ambassador to Japan; the significance of his appointment is not lost on the Japanese. It is an indication that President Carter sees Japan as a most important ally and a leading world power; Mansfield himself has advocated that Japan and American both recognize the postwar era is over and begin a new and equal partnership.

The problems facing the two countries are many and various— trade, energy, China, Korea, Russia—but few people are better suited for the task of coordinating their discussions than Mansfield. He brings international experience, a prodigious knowledge of Asia, a feel for negotiation, and, perhaps most important, a sense of decency that reflects America's and Japan's best hopes for the future.

Mike Mansfield's retirement did not last long at all. This in itself is a tribute to the boy from such a humble background who, in 1917, confided to his sisters that he wanted to join the Navy and see the world.

WILLIAM D. JAMES
Executive Editor
Great Falls (Montana) *Tribune*

PHOTO ESSAY

With wife, Maureen

Wide World Photo

With President Carter and Vice-President Mondale

At play with Senators Kennedy and Jackson, 1954

Visiting with President Carter in the Oval Office

Sewing a button on his coat at the Great Falls, Montana,
airport, en route to Japan

THE END OF THE POSTWAR ERA

Time for a New Partnership
of Equality with Japan

The four reports contained in this volume were presented by Sen. Mike Mansfield to the Committee on Foreign Relations, United States Senate, 94th Congress, 2nd session, in 1976.

LETTER OF TRANSMITTAL

AUGUST 2, 1976.

Hon. JOHN SPARKMAN,
Chairman, Committee on Foreign Relations,
U.S. Senate, Washington, D.C.

DEAR MR. CHAIRMAN: As you know, with the Committee's permission, during the July recess I made an official trip to Japan to study major United States foreign and security problems in the Far East with emphasis on United States relations with Japan and Japanese attitudes concerning a number of matters of mutual interest, such as issues involving the People's Republic of China, the Soviet Union, and Korea. I am hereby transmitting my report on that trip. A confidential report has been sent to the President.

I was in Japan from July 9 through July 16, when I returned to Washington. While there I received a thorough briefing from Ambassador James D. Hodgson and his staff concerning political, economic, and security matters. I also had an informative briefing from Lt. General Walter T. Galligan, USAF, Commander, U.S. Forces Japan, and his staff concerning the status of U.S. military bases and personnel in Japan. Both Ambassador Hodgson and General Galligan were most helpful and cooperative.

I met with a number of officials of the Japanese government, each of whom was most generous with his time. Among those with whom I held discussions were Prime Minister Takeo Miki; Deputy Prime Minister and Director General of Economic Planning, Takeo Fukuda; Foreign Minister Kiichi Miyazawa; Director General of the Japan Defense Agency, Michata Sakata; and Finance Minister Masayoshi Ohira. My conversations with each official covered a wide range of subjects and thus gave me a broad cross section of opinion within the Japanese government on many matters of common interest.

In addition to these meetings, I had an opportunity for informal discussions with Deputy Minister of Foreign Affairs Keisuke Arita and several of his colleagues, former Japanese Ambassadors to the United States Takeshi Yasukawa and Nobuhiko Ushiba, and others.

I was accompanied on the trip by Mr. Francis R. Valeo, Secretary of the Senate, and Mr. Norvill Jones of the Committee staff. In order to obtain further information concerning the Korean problems and the Taiwan issues, as they relate to Japan, I sent Mr. Valeo to Korea and Mr. Jones to Taiwan following the completion of my schedule in Japan. At my request, Mr. Jones also inspected the U.S. military base situation in Okinawa on his way back to Washington.

I wish to express my appreciation to the Department of State for making my travel arrangements; to Ambassador Hodgson and his staff for their assistance and many courtesies; to General Galligan and his staff for the briefing and other helpful information; to the Congressional Research Service of the Library of Congress for assembling background materials; to the Department of Defense for assistance in the field to Mr. Valeo and Mr. Jones; to Mr. Valeo, who, as a former consultant to the Committee on Foreign Relations, has accompanied me on many past missions abroad, and to Mr. Jones of the Committee staff, who has also accompanied me on a number of past missions, for their assistance in connection with the trip.

Sincerely yours,

MIKE MANSFIELD.

THE END OF THE POSTWAR ERA—TIME FOR A NEW PARTNERSHIP OF EQUALITY WITH JAPAN

I. IMPORTANCE OF THE UNITED STATES-JAPAN RELATIONSHIP

One hundred and twenty-three years ago Commodore Matthew Perry led four U.S. naval vessels into Tokyo Bay, opening Japan to the outside world after more than two centuries of isolation. A new relationship began for our two countries, a relationship which, over the years, has moved through a broad spectrum, from friendship to war and back to friendship again. It is commonplace to say that there is a special relationship between our two countries. But this is an inadequate term to describe the interdependence and mutuality of interests that have come to bind our countries together. A stable Japan, which poses no military threat to the nations of Asia, is essential to stability and peace in the Pacific and the world. Although it lacks military power, Japan is the world's third ranking economic power and second only to the United States among the industrial democracies. In this sense, it is a factor to be reckoned with in its capacity to influence the flow of international events.

Aside from the umbrella of security provided by the mutual security treaty, the United States relationship is essential to Japan as a source of food, raw materials, and as a market for Japan's industrial output. To the United States, far less dependent on world markets for economic well-being, the Japanese tie is essential in a different, but no less important sense. It is a fundamental pillar in present U.S. foreign policy whose goal is continued stability in the Western Pacific. Geography and history, combined with the genius and industry of the Japanese people, have made Japan a keystone of that policy. The waters of the Pacific lap the shores of all the world's major powers—the United States, the Soviet Union, China, and Japan—and it is in the environs of the latter country that the interests of all are most entwined. For this nation which has fought three wars in Asia within a generation, the role of Japan in the structure of peace in the Pacific will continue to be of utmost importance in the years ahead. It is in the interest of both peoples to work at strengthening this unique relationship.

The visit by Commodore Perry began what became the first of a series of ups and downs in relations between Japan and the United States. Unlike our ties with Great Britain, language and cultural differences have been obstacles to mutual understanding between Japanese and Americans. Trust does not come easy under these circumstances. Extraordinary efforts by both sides are necessary. As Professor Edwin Reischauer, former U.S. Ambassador to Japan, wrote recently, this difficulty is compounded by the fact that: "We for our part have lingering traces of the unquestioned nineteenth century assumption that the West was in all ways superior to the rest of the world."

Since the post-World War II occupation began, Americans have had a tendency to take the Japanese tie for granted. The Nixon "shocks" arising out of a failure to consult on measures to support the dollar, to suspend soybean exports, and on the new China policy have not been forgotten. There should be no more such unnecessary and undiplomatic treatment of our closest major ally in the Pacific.

II. FOREIGN POLICY AND SECURITY

Japan is an island nation. That, and an astute foreign policy have relieved its people of any discernible fear of attack from abroad. It enjoys good relations with all of the major powers and diplomatic and commercial relations with practically every nation of the world. A security commitment from the United States permits the spending of less than one percent of its gross national product for defense purposes. Japan's foreign policy, which is built around the umbrella of the security pact with the United States, has paid rich dividends by freeing resources for economic growth that would otherwise be devoted to unproductive military spending.

Article IX of the Japanese Constitution is the foundation of Japan's external policies. It states:

Aspiring sincerely to an international peace based on justice and order, the Japanese people forever renounce war as a sovereign right of the nation and the threat or use of force as means of settling international disputes.

In order to accomplish the aim of the preceding paragraph, land, sea and air forces, as well as other war potential, will never be maintained. The right of belligerency of the state will not be recognized.

Within these constraints, Japan has, like a Phoenix, risen from the ashes of defeat and humiliation into a unique position on the international scene. There is widespread public sensitivity among the Japanese to all military issues, particularly to those involving nuclear weapons. Japan's status as an unarmed, economic giant in a world bristling with weapons of mass destruction has contributed greatly to the easing of bitter memories of Japanese militarism, to the opening of doors to Japanese economic dynamism, and to a more stable international environment, notably in Northeast Asia.

Japan maintains only a small Self-Defense Force consisting of some 240,000 men. Recruitment for even this small force is difficult. At bottom, Japan's real security, aside from the U.S. commitment, is entrusted to effective foreign policies.

Following in the path of the Nixon visit to Peking, Japan established diplomatic relations with the People's Republic of China on September 29, 1972, but a Sino-Japanese peace treaty to end the formal state of hostilities from World War II has not yet been concluded. It is stalled by a dispute over Chinese insistence on an "anti-hegemony" clause. Although agreeable in principle to such a clause, the Japanese confront the fact that the Soviet Union has indicated that such language in a treaty would be considered an unfriendly act. Negotiations with China have been at a stalemate since last year. Meanwhile, trade and other relations with China continue, with $2.5 billion in exports to China and $1.5 billion in imports from China in 1975, three times the level of trade in 1970.

Under the "Japanese formula," Japan also maintains economic and cultural relations with Taiwan. The nation's interests on Taiwan are represented by the unofficial organization designated the "Japanese Interchange Association," which is headed by a former Japanese ambassador. The association is financed primarily by private funds. Taiwan's interests in Japan are represented by the Far East Association. The personnel of neither organization have any form of diplomatic status or immunity.

Other countries which recognize the People's Republic of China look after their trade or cultural interests in Taiwan through varying types of organizations: Great Britain through the Anglo-Taiwan Trade Committee; Germany through the Goethe Institution; Spain through the Cervantes Center; and the Philippines through the Asian Exchange Center. Taiwan has developed a web of relationships in order to handle specific circumstances which may be involved with any individual country.

The "Japanese formula" has worked well for Japan. Since formal diplomatic recognition of the People's Republic of China, trade, investment, and travel between Taiwan and Japan have all expanded. Trade has more than doubled—to $2.5 billion last year—and accounts for 22 percent of all Taiwan's trade (the U.S. accounted for 31 percent of Taiwan's trade in 1975—$3.47 billion).

With regard to the Soviet Union, Japan has yet to conclude a World War II peace treaty, the matter being snagged over four islands north of Hokkaido claimed by both Japan and the Soviet Union.[1] No break in the impasse is in sight. There is in Sapporo, the principal city of Hokkaido, a "Movement for the Reversion of the Habomais." The agitation which this group fosters from time to time is tempered by the realization that the Soviet Union is in a position to curtail fishing rights which are of significance to the Japanese. Moreover, there is a substantial general trade with the Soviet Union, although it is somewhat less than commerce with China. Last year exports to the U.S.S.R. were $1.62 billion and imports $1.17 billion. With regard to the status of Japanese joint ventures with the Soviets in the development of Siberia, many projects have been discussed but only two, natural gas and timber, have made progress. Others seem to be "fading away," as one Japanese official put it, due in part apparently, to the reluctance of U.S. private interests, which were also involved, to pursue them at this time.

Japanese officials are concerned about the increase in Soviet naval activities in the Western Pacific, citing in particular an increase in the activities of intelligence vessels. While I was in Japan, Soviet ships and ASW aircraft were conducting maneuvers in the Okinawa area. Insofar as Japan is concerned, the increase in Soviet naval operations in the Western Pacific is viewed, one involved official said, as constituting "a potential threat to Japan—but it is not overt yet." He went on to say that the Soviets were also engaged in a "cultural offensive."

Developments in the situation on the Korean Peninsula are reflected in Japan, in part, through the large Korean community in Japan, which is divided in its sentiments about the problems of the Peninsula.

---

[1] The Islands in dispute are: Etorofu, Kunashiri, Shikotan, and Habomai.

Some favor the North and others support South Korea and Japan is frequently drawn into difficulties arising from this division. There is also a deep-seated historic concern in Japan with the impact of developments in Korea on Japanese security.

The traditional overland invasion route to Japan has been via the Peninsula. While this route has also operated in the other direction, the fact is that in present circumstances both Soviet and Chinese military power which might approach by way of Korea appear overwhelming to Japan. Those Japanese given to nightmares in this matter, moreover, note that if the Koreans of the North and South should ever get together, their combined armed strengths would be four or five times greater than Japan's lightly armed self-defense force.

It is clear that a military conflict between North and South Korea could pose a threat to Japan especially if it were to draw in great powers as would be almost inevitable. Indeed, a breakdown of order in South Korea alone would create serious difficulties for the Japanese who have developed a major trading relationship of about $4 billion annually with Seoul [2] and, in addition, have large investments in Korea.[3]

There is little that is apparent in the current Korean situation to feed these Japanese anxieties. The Republic of Korea, functions under a government which is for all practical purposes, a military-bureaucratic authoritarianism under the control of President Park Chung-Hee. Two years ago there was still protest and agitation for political freedom on the part of intellectuals, religious groups and others but that has now ceased. Civil liberties are in abeyance and fear of prison or death has silenced the opposition. The Park Administration is said to have considerable popular support. Certainly, it has the backing of the military establishment and the acquiesence if not the active support of major industrial and commercial groups. It has, of course, official support from the United States and, probably, from other foreign sources. The government, in short, gives the appearance of stability.

Moreover, the South Korean economy has been converted into a modern establishment which is second only to Japan among Asian nations. Its peoples are industrious and dexterous and, in the space of two decades, have developed a great range of modern industrial skills. Recent concentration on the improvement of agriculture has resulted in a rapid growth in the output of food to a point that is now close to adequate for maintaining the population.

Presently, the nation is in the midst of a boom, with industrial production expanding at the rate of 20 percent a year. The growth in GNP is running between 6 percent and 8 percent which, in the face of a drastically declining birth rate, is said to be bringing a great improvement in general living standards.

The Korean economic transition has depended heavily on U.S. economic aid, a program which is drawing to a close. The vestiges are calculated at about $40 million in the pipeline and, approximately $300

---

[2] Japan also has very limited trading contacts with North Korea, which, for the present have been suspended due to the inability of Pyongyang to make payment for past purchases.

[3] One readily recognizable yardstick of this investment; all black and white Sony T/Vs which are distributed by Japan are now made in South Korea.

million in agricultural products, under a PL 480 agreement. An investment guarantee program continues to operate and is a significant factor in the inflow of private capital.

Korean trade is still closely tied to the United States and Japan, with the latter, in particular, providing a funnel for the outflow of Korean manufactures. However, the Koreans are beginning to develop independent commercial contacts with the rest of the world and Korean firms are said to have written in the neighborhood of $2 billion of contracts to undertake construction in the Middle Eastern oil countries. Seoul is attracting an increasing inflow of businessmen from that region and from all other parts of the world, except Latin America and Africa.

The Korean capital city which now contains about 7 million persons is the center of industrial and commercial activity. It is a dynamic modern city in the midst of a building boom. It should be noted that the building includes deep concrete tunnels everywhere which are designed to relieve heavy surface traffic but which could serve as shelters in the event of war.

It is not possible to find in the present situation a persuasive reason to believe that war is imminent. Along the 38° parallel, except for occasional localized personnel clashes and a two-way loud-speaker propaganda war, all is quiet. The International Commission (Czechoslovakia, Poland, Switzerland and Sweden), as it has been for more than two decades, is present in the Zone. North Koreans and U.S. and South Korean military personnel continue to maintain rigidly formal contact, with occasional quarrels across the conference table that stand astride the 38° parallel. While the southern approaches to the demilitarized zone run through a kind of no-man's land, it is said that 40,000 tourists and other visitors a year pass through them to the 38° parallel. North Korea also has its flow of tourist buses carrying Koreans and other visitors from Communist countries to observe the dividing line.

The Soviet Union and the People's Republic of China are believed to have exercised a restraining influence on Pyongyang in order to prevent a precipitous rekindling of the war. However, Kim Il-sung, the Northern ruler, asserts that there is no intention to seek unification of the country by military means. The two sides continue to meet periodically at a very low level of Red Cross contact to seek unification by other means but progress to date has been completely absent.

In the South, the government stresses continuously the danger of invasion from the North and concentrates on the improvement of its military forces. The modernization program, except in regard to the Navy, is well-advanced. The U.S. aid-subsidy of the Korean military establishment is now largely provided under the military purchase program. The Koreans are assuming an increasingly larger share of the cost of their military establishment.

Notwithstanding these developments, the presence of U.S. combat forces in the South is seen as the critical factor in preventing an invasion from the North. There is deployed in the South, a contingent of about 40,000 U.S. servicemen. Except for small economy-induced reductions, the number has not been lowered in many years. Even those who stress most heavily the role of these forces in preventing a renewal of conflict do not argue that the total cannot be reduced in a gradual way over a period of years or, even, eventually be withdrawn. Any suggestion of rapid withdrawal, however, is a source of profound anxiety to South Korean officials, even more perhaps than to the Japanese. Some estimates are that the present structure in South Korea would have no more than a 50–50 chance of survival without the U.S. military presence. However, the Administration has made clear that the United States has no intention of withdrawing precipitously and, similarly, the Congress has not taken any measures which would compel a precipitous withdrawal. In short, the situation insofar as the U.S. forces are concerned is one of stability.

It is a stability, however, which is underlain with uncertainties. In the first place, the economic progress which is probably a mainstay of public acquiescence in the present government rests on an extremely fragile base. It is dependent almost entirely on the import of raw materials and the export of industrial surpluses which are produced competitively largely by the comparative advantage of a low wage scale and investment guarantees. Any tremors in either the economy of Japan or the United States tend to become earthquakes in South Korea.

In the second place, although the present government is fully aware of the aversion which exists in segments of Congressional and other opinion in the United States regarding its authoritarianism, it appears to have no intention of modifying the present political structure. Its view is that this structure is not only necessary for defense against the North but is essential to the kind of economic progress which is being fostered in the South.

Finally, there is the question of U.S. military withdrawal. The question is often asked: how long will the commitment last? Clearly, a precipitous pullout by the United States, even if it did not open the door to military attack from the North would shake the government of South Korea to its very foundations. The reactions of an embittered political opposition and from within the military establishment are not measurable. Moreover, it is entirely possible that the deep-seated sentiments for Korean unification would surface in both North and South. The potential for spreading instability would be very great. Notwithstanding outward appearances, then, the basis for the Japanese concern regarding the Korean Peninsula is very real. In short, Korea is a time-bomb which has yet to be defused.

Looking at Asia in general, there is a strong mutuality of interests shared by Japan and the United States. Japan is a firm supporter of ASEAN, the Association of Southeast Asian Nations, as a new force for economic cooperation and progress in Southeast Asia. Japan is also interested in working toward broadening the regional concept of ASEAN to bring the nations of Indochina into the current membership: the Philippines, Thailand, Malaysia, Singapore, and Indonesia. Regional cooperation for peaceful purposes is a concept which appears to have broad support in Japan and, if pursued, should contribute to Asian stability and progress. "Poverty and peace," one Japanese official put it, "cannot co-exist."

As to national security matters, in June the Japanese Defense Agency issued a Defense White Paper, the second since the end of World War II. The basic objectives of the paper were to stimulate discussion of Japan's defense posture and to strengthen public support for the Government's program to upgrade the quality of these forces.

The report is premised on a continuation of the international status quo between the United States, the Soviet Union, and China and no change in Japan's ultimate dependence on the U.S. security guarantee.

Basically, the report takes an optimistic view of the international situation for Japan and assumes that any U.S.–U.S.S.R. conflict will not spill over to affect Japan. It rejects a nuclear option, stating that:

> If Japan should take a nuclear option, even for a purely defensive purpose, her actual possession of nuclear arms will create serious suspicion and fear on the part of other nations.

The international environment on which Japan's defense policy will be based is described as assuming:

> (a) that the U.S. and the Soviet Union will try to avoid an inter-continental nuclear war and an armed conflict which might lead to their full-scale involvement.
> (b) that the Soviet Union will continue to face many European problems— a NATO-Warsaw Pact confrontation and the control of East European nations, among other matters.
> (c) that Sino-Soviet relations, if improved partially, will most unlikely lead to an end of confrontation.
> (d) that in Sino-U.S. relations, a further adjustment will continue on a reciprocal basis, and
> (e) that the status quo, more or less, will be maintained in the Korean Peninsula where a minor incident would not escalate to a large-scale conflict.

Japan's view of the U.S.-Japan security relationship is described this way:

> (a) The system is generally understood to play the role of preventing aggression against Japan from actually taking place, and of limiting the scale of an invasion, should it ever be undertaken.
> (b) The system is also instrumental in providing the U.S. forces with facilities and areas for their use, which in turn make their presence tenable.
> An integral part of the basic framework of international relations in Asia, the system thus contributes to the stability of the world and the maintenance of peace. Finally, but not the least importantly, it is the indispensable base of the wider spectrum of friendly U.S.-Japanese relations.

Clearly, reliance on the U.S. commitment remains strong on the part of the Japanese government, and close observers say that there is less controversy now over the U.S. security treaty than at any time since the relationship was formalized twenty-four years ago. There is now a more rational, less emotional, public dialogue over security issues than in the past. I found no indication that the fall of Indochina had resulted in any lessened confidence in the U.S. commitment, although there was some initial nervousness.

The White Paper emphasizes that Japan's defense objective is "on qualitative improvement rather than on quantitative expansion in the planned buildup of our defense capability." Defense Minister Sakata described the basic concept, as one for a "small armed force, but a bigger load" for Japan. The Japanese view, in this connection, should be respected. It behooves us to be very cautious in taking any step that could be interpreted by Asians, or by the Japanese people, as pressing the Japanese government to make a quantitative increase in the size of its defense force or to change its defense posture in a significant way.

This year Japan will spend .089 percent of its GNP and 6.17 percent of the government budget for defense, compared with current defense spending totaling 5.5 percent of GNP and 24.8 percent of the budget by the United States. Japan ranks tenth in the world in military spending but at the bottom in relation to per capita income, GNP, or as a portion of the overall budget.

Agreement has been reached to establish a joint Defense Cooperation Subcommittee to operate under the U.S.-Japan Consultative Committee on Security, the basic focal point for discussion of security treaty matters. The Subcommittee will have the responsibility to discuss guidelines for military cooperation between the two countries in the event of an emergency. Officials on both sides place much value on the new subcommittee, seeing it as a symbol of a new spirit of cooperation on security matters.

A. U.S. bases and personnel

United States bases in Japan, particularly those on Okinawa, are still a source of tension although the situation is easing with continued reduction in the number of bases and the drawdown of military personnel.[4]

Article VI of the U.S.-Japan Security Treaty provides:

For the purpose of contributing to the security of Japan and the maintenance of international peace and security in the Far East, the United States of America is granted the use by its land, aid and naval forces of facilities and areas in Japan.

In 1952, according to the Japan Defense Agency, there were 2,824 U.S. military facilities in Japan, of all sizes, covering 334,100 acres, and occupied by 260,000 U.S. servicemen. These facilities have now been reduced to 136 and take up 125,089 acres; they range in significance from the huge Kadena Air Base on Okinawa to a single antenna site taking less than an acre. Most are small facilities with few people attached. There are still 50,000 U.S. servicemen in Japan, along with 43,220 dependents and 3,768 civilian Department of Defense employees. Land for the bases is provided rent-free. The rent on privately owned land is paid to the landowner by the Japanese government. Thirty-eight of the facilities are used jointly by U.S. forces and the Japanese Self-Defense Forces. More than half of the base acreage and nearly two-thirds of the personnel are located on Okinawa. Other than those on Okinawa, measured by the number of personnel attached, there are only seven major U.S. bases:

	U.S. military personnel attached
1. Yokota Air Base—Headquarters, U.S. Forces Japan and of the 5th Air Force	4,122
2. Camp Zama—Headquarters of the U.S. Army in Japan	791
3. Yokosuka—Headquarters, U.S. Naval Forces in Japan	1,876
4. Iwakuni Air Station—Air Base for First Marine Air Wing	5,102
5. Atsugi Naval Air Facility—7th Fleet Naval Air Facility	614
6. Misawa Air Base—Air Force Base	3,081
7. Sasebo—Naval base	168

---

[4] What has happened on the northern island of Hokkaido is a microcosm of the kind of contraction in the U.S. presence in most parts of Japan over the last quarter of a century. At the end of World War II, the military occupation introduced 13,000 U.S. troops into Hokkaido, mostly centered on the capital city of Sapporo. At least a division remained during the Korean War. In 1959, the airfield for Sapporo reverted to Japan and U.S. forces were cut back to a communications unit. By 1970, only a guard unit of 200 men remained. It was not until June of 1975 that this unit was withdrawn. What is left of the U.S. military presence is a Coast Guard "LORAN" unit on the Hokkaido coast. The official U.S. presence now consists of a consulate in Sapporo, with three Americans, a U.S.I.S. center run by an American and a specialist from the Department of Agriculture, on a temporary basis.

Japan makes a significant financial contribution to paying for the costs of the U.S. military presence. This year Japan will pay $373 million toward the costs of retaining the bases: $105 million for land rental, $104 million in compensation to impacted communities, and $173 million for the costs of reducing the number of bases through consolidation. All new construction in connection with the consolidation of U.S. facilities is paid for by the Japanese government.

1. Okinawa.—Although anti-U.S. military base pressures on the Japanese mainland seem to have eased, there is still strong public opposition to American bases on Okinawa. Twenty percent of the land area of the island of Okinawa is occupied by U.S. bases and they take up to 12% of the Ryukyu Islands chain. A joint decision was reached recently to return twelve additional U.S. facilities, including a firing range on Iejima Island which has been the source of much local controversy. After these reversions take place, the area occupied by the U.S. bases will be reduced from 12 percent to 9.8 percent of the total land area of the island chain.

Okinawans have strong feelings about the bases, which are scattered throughout the island in a checkerboard fashion. Residents carry a bitter legacy of anti-military feeling as a residue from World War II, when 150,000 Okinawans were killed. There is also a widespread feeling that Okinawans are carrying a disproportionate burden of Japan's defense effort, that they are being used in Tokyo. They are also concerned over the possibility of being sucked into an outside war regardless of the fact that they do not feel threatened by any external power.

Recently the opposition candidate for governor won in a close election with a plank that called for removal of all U.S. bases and personnel, although the pro-Tokyo government candidate also favored substantial reductions. It is impossible to determine how significant a factor the differences in the views of the candidates on the bases was in the election, but officials in Tokyo with whom I discussed the situation were acutely aware of the sensitivity of the base issue to Okinawans. It is an issue easily susceptible to political exploitation throughout Japan.

Although the bases account for 15 percent or more of Okinawa's income, this fact does not appear to have softened the persistent public resentment against the U.S. military presence. The 32,000 remaining servicemen in their concentrated U.S. communities still stick out like a sore thumb on the island, although incidents of overt personal hostility are becoming rarer. It is interesting to note that there are only about 5,000 members of the Japanese Self-Defense Force on Okinawa, using land which totals less than one percent of the area used by American forces. There is little joint use of facilities; the Japanese air units, for example, do not have a firing range and must return to the Japanese mainland for firing practice.

Apart from Okinawa, a heavy U.S. military concentration exists in the Tokyo–Yokohama area, the most densely populated part of Japan and is being reduced only slowly. The Sanno Hotel which has been held by the U.S. Army since occupation days is an example. Located in the heart of Tokyo, the hotel is used primarily for U.S. military personnel on leave and, on occasion, by U.S. Government travelers on military business. Since the mid-1950's the Japanese government and the owners of the property have been trying to get the United States to release this building. Finally, late last year, after taking the Japanese government to court, the owner won a settlement calling for payment of compensation and for return of the property within five years. But the U.S. still insists on a replacement in the downtown Tokyo area before it will relinquish the Sanno, notwithstanding the fact that any valid military justification for retaining this particular facility ended long ago.

The reduction and consolidation of U.S. bases in Japan which is spurred by pressures of budget limitations, steeply-climbing prices in Japan, and Japanese cooperation, is generally headed in the right direction. It should continue, on the basis of close consultation at all times with Japanese officials.

III. ECONOMIC RELATIONS

Japanese and American economic interests are inextricably entwined. America is Japan's largest market and Japan is our most important market, aside from Canada. Currently the United States absorbs some 24 percent of Japan's exports, down from a considerably higher proportion several years ago, marking the diversification of Japan's foreign markets.

There have, of course, been problems with our trade in the past—over steel, textiles and other items—but with time, restraint, and concessions on both sides these problems have been surmounted. Other bilateral trade difficulties are to be anticipated in the future. With goodwill, cooperation, and understanding of mutual needs, these problems should also be manageable. There may well be a need for additional mechanisms for day-to-day dialogue between the two governments on economic issues, both to find solutions to problems before they become critical as well as to provide forums for discussion of matters of mutual interest.

A matter of potential concern for the immediate future, is the reappearance of a growing gap in bilateral trade balances. Japanese exports to the United States for January–April 1976 exceeded imports from the United States by $1.628 billion, compared with a deficit of $735.5 million for the last four months of 1975.

Japan's economic growth rate this year, in real terms, is estimated at 6.2 percent which will result in a GNP of $515.6 billion, somewhat more than one-third of that of the United States. Inflation has been brought under reasonable control and is now running at an annual rate of 8.8 percent. Unemployment is 2 percent, although U.S. and Japanese figures are not comparable due to different employment practices. Environmental issues are of growing public concern in Japan and expenditures for environmental protection now absorb some 13 percent of all capital expenditures compared with about 5 percent for comparable spending in the United States.

As is the case with most other raw materials, Japan is heavily dependent for its energy requirements on foreign sources and it will continue to be for the foreseeable future. Eighty-nine percent of its energy needs are derived from imports (seventy-seven percent from oil). Under a ten-year plan for energy development, its dependence on foreign energy sources will be reduced by only seven percent. Japan's domestic petroleum production is negligible, although some drilling is underway at offshore sites.

Other than the trade deficit, which to a great extent is a factor of the uneven recovery rates of our respective economies, there are only two major bilateral issues of current concern, fisheries and air routes. The Japanese people depend on fish for 60 percent of their protein and are heavily dependent on ocean fishery resources. They are deeply concerned over the potential impact of the recently enacted law to establish a 200 mile territorial limit for fishing (P.L. 94–265). I explained to the officials who raised this matter that the Congress voted this interim measure out of self-defense following repeated failures by the United Nations Law of the Sea Conference to arrive at an international agreement; after many nations had unilaterally increased their territorial claims to 200 miles; and that imposition of the limit would be held in abeyance for an additional period to give the U.N. Conference more time to come up with a solution. Discussions between Japanese and U.S. officials over the implementation of the new law have begun and it is to be hoped that a satisfactory bilateral solution can be found, assuming that the U.N. Conference again fails to produce an international accord. The air route issue involves a Japanese desire for new ports of entry into the United States and it is also likely to involve requests by U.S. airlines for the right to continue service to Okinawa.

The Lockheed affair, or Lockheed "typhoon," as one official called it, is Japan's Watergate. It is a Japanese—not an American—problem. Thus far, it appears that the affair has had no major adverse effect on Japan-U.S. relations. However, it has had an impact on the conscience of the Japanese public and may eventually set in motion significant changes in Japan's political structure and alinement. In my judgment, the American political system has not only survived the Watergate affair, in the end, it may be strengthened by it. It is entirely possible that the Lockheed scandal could have the same effect in Japan.

The Senate Committee on Foreign Relations has turned over to the Executive Branch all information in its possession relating to the affair for transmittal to the Japanese government. Japanese officials are aware that Congress had been fully cooperative with their government on the matter.

Looking to the future, it is in the interest of Japan, the United States, and the world to establish international ground rules to control under-the-table business dealings and political manipulations like those involved in the Lockheed affair. In this era of multinational corporations and state trading, a single country cannot do much, acting alone, to prevent such practices. "Multinational firms," one Japanese official agreed, "cannot be checked through individual governments." This dry rot in the world's commerce is an international problem and solutions in a similar fashion can only be international. The United Nations may well be peculiarly suited to this purpose.

IV. CONCLUDING OBSERVATIONS

Although the Japan-U.S. relationship began nearly a century and a quarter ago, the unique meshing of our two countries' interests began with the end of World War II. Japan has now become the second most powerful industrial democracy in the world. And under the U.S. security umbrella, Japan has been free of fear of outside attack and of burdensome military spending. It has been able to devote its vast energies to creating an economic machine of immense productivity.

In 1960, riots and widespread public protests against the mutual security treaty with the United States caused the cancellation of President Eisenhower's plans to visit Japan. President Ford's visit to Japan in 1974 and Emperor Hirohito's visit to the United States last October, historic occasions for both nations, epitomized the changes which have taken place in our relationship since that time. At no period in our post-war history have U.S. relations with Japan been better.

But as the visit by Commodore Perry signaled the end of one era for Japan, an era of isolation from the outside world, we have entered a new era in our contemporary relationship. The end of the post-war era was signaled by the 1972 Okinawa reversion agreement. We have now reached a new plateau, where trust in affairs of mutual concern is essential to both countries. We cannot afford either to preach to the Japanese, to patronize them, or to ignore their legitimate interests. The only basis for trust is to treat with one another on the basis of equality.

The U.S.-Japan security treaty is more than a pledge to maintain a stable and peaceful Pacific. It is a symbol of the need for day-to-day cooperation between Japan and the United States across a range of human activities. The partnership begun at the end of World War II should be strengthened by additional mechanisms for consultation and discussion, building on the precedent of the recently created Joint Defense Cooperation Subcommittee.

Japan is the only major nation in the world which has rejected military power as the basis for the protection and advancement of its interests. Japan is in a unique position, therefore, to exercise leadership in dealing with the problems which will increasingly trouble the world in the years ahead. Environmental issues, shortages of energy and other resources, food and population problems, the world arms burden and nuclear dangers—all are matters with regard to which Japan is uniquely situated to play an international role of leadership. Japan's unique position in the world warrants a permanent seat on the United Nations Security Council and an amendment to the U.N. Charter to that end would be in order.

There may be shifts in Japanese political currents in the period ahead as Japan goes through a period of reassessment. It is especially important that United States officials become better acquainted with and more closely attuned to the broader spectrum of Japanese opinion. A greater exchange of academicians, politicians, journalists, cultural leaders, and others would be in the longrange interests of both countries.

Japanese and American policy interests in the Far East are well served by continuation of the present security treaty relationship. Japanese confidence in the United States commitment is a key factor for stability in the area. I found no evidence of a move to change Japan's military status in such a way as to cause her neighbors concern. Nor is there any reason that a further reduction in U.S. bases and forces should create uncertainty about the U.S. treaty commitment. Continuation of the present policy to consolidate and eliminate non-essential facilities is desirable, economical and will serve our common interests.

U.S.-Japan relations are good but they could be better. The era of patron-client is over. A new relationship on the basis of equality and a mutuality of interests has begun. Professor Edwin Reischauer described the potential of that relationship as a pattern for the world's future in this way:

> If we and the Japanese can build a fully equal relationship of complete trust and cooperation as the two leading members of the group of industrialized democracies, this may be a hopeful sign that in time other such relationships can be built across the chasms of racial and cultural difference, as we move toward creating a truly viable "one world."

This is a worthy goal for both countries.

V. RECOMMENDATIONS

The recommendations which are contained in this report may be summarized as follows:

1. No more "shocks". Wherever feasible, joint mechanisms should be established for periodic consultations on problems of common concern. Our unique relationship warrants unique approaches to insure a continuing dialogue, at all levels, on matters of mutual interest.

2. Japan should obtain a permanent seat on the U.N. Security Council.

3. The reduction and consolidation of U.S. military facilities and personnel should continue in close consultation with the Japanese government.

4. There should be broadened contacts, official and unofficial, between Japan and the United States.

5. The United Nations should undertake to develop a treaty encompassing a code of conduct for international commercial dealings which would outlaw practices such as those involved in the Lockheed affair.

6. There should be a gradual withdrawal of U.S. ground forces from South Korea as that nation's military strength improves.

POSTWAR SOUTHEAST ASIA

A Search for Neutrality
and Independence

LETTER OF TRANSMITTAL

AUGUST 31, 1976.

Hon. JOHN SPARKMAN,
Chairman, Committee on Foreign Relations,
U.S. Senate, Washington, D.C.

DEAR MR. CHAIRMAN: With the Committee's permission, during the August recess I made an official trip to Thailand, Burma and Laos to study various aspects of United States relations with those countries and regional developments which bear on American policy questions. I also stopped in Hong Kong to obtain a briefing from the staff of the American Consulate General concerning the current situation in the People's Republic of China and information about the international traffic in narcotics. Enroute to and returning from Southeast Asia, I also stopped briefly in Tokyo to receive up-to-date reports on recent political developments in Japan.

I am hereby transmitting my report on the trip, in the form of a speech I made in the Senate on August 26.

In Thailand I met with His Majesty King Phumiphon Adunyadet, Prime Minister Seni Pramot, Foreign Minister Phichai Rattakun and other officials of the foreign ministry. Ambassador Charles S. Whitehouse provided me with a thorough briefing.

From Bangkok, I flew in a small airplane, attached to the U.S. Embassy in Thailand, to Vientiane, Laos, the first U.S. aircraft allowed into Laos in more than a year. While in Laos, I had a discussion with Deputy Foreign Minister Khamphay Boupha, received a briefing from Mr. Thomas Corcoran, Charge d'Affaires of the U.S. Embassy, and his staff, and had an opportunity to meet informally with a number of foreign diplomats and other observers of the Laotian scene.

I then travelled to Rangoon, Burma. President Ne Win was out of the country and, in his absence, I met with General San Yu, Secretary of the Council of State, and a number of other Burmese officials. Ambassador David L. Osborn and members of his staff were helpful in many ways during my stay in Burma.

I wish to express my appreciation to United States officials at each of the posts I visited for the assistance they provided, to the Department of State for making my travel arrangements, to the Library of Congress for assembling background materials, and to Mr. Francis Valeo, Secretary of the Senate, and Mr. Norvill Jones, of the staff of the Committee on Foreign Relations, both of whom have accompanied me on a number of past missions, for their assistance in connection with the trip.

Sincerely,

MIKE MANSFIELD.

POSTWAR SOUTHEAST ASIA—A SEARCH FOR NEUTRALITY AND INDEPENDENCE

SPEECH BY SENATOR MIKE MANSFIELD IN THE UNITED STATES SENATE, AUGUST 26, 1976

Mr. MANSFIELD. Mr. President, 1 year ago, on behalf of the Committee on Foreign Relations, I visited three nations in Southeast Asia, Thailand, the Philippines, and Burma, to study regional and local developments after the ending of U.S. involvement in Indochina. Upon my return, I reported to the committee that:

> Throughout Southeast Asia, nations are now making reassessments of their relationships. Nationalism and neutrality, mixed with a budding interest in regional cooperation, are the driving forces at work.

I ask unanimous consent that pertinent portions of this report be printed in the Record following my remarks.

The ACTING PRESIDENT pro tempore. Without objection, it is so ordered.

(See exhibit 1, p. 11.)

Mr. MANSFIELD. During the recent congressional recess, I returned to Southeast Asia to make an up-to-date reappraisal of the situation there, visiting Thailand, Burma, and Laos. A confidential report has already been submitted to the President as a result of that trip. This is my report to the Senate.

Winds of change still sweep the area, continuing to move the region toward cohesion and an easing of tensions. The U.S. role in this movement is limited and must remain so. It is not for this Nation, nor is it possible for this Nation to tell the nations of Southeast Asia what is in their interest. If we have learned anything from our sad experience in Indochina, it is that the future of Southeast Asia is for the nations of the area to decide and without outside interference.

The Philippines, Thailand, Malaysia, Singapore, and Indonesia, through the Association of Southeast Asian Nations, ASEAN, have taken small but positive steps toward regional cooperation. In February, the heads of state of the five ASEAN members met at their first summit conference to produce a treaty of amity and cooperation and other agreements looking toward closer collaboration on problems of common concern. There remained, however, an uneasy uncertainty about what course Vietnam, now a powerful, unified nation of 40 million people, would take in regional affairs.

Twenty-two years after the Geneva cease-fire agreement which temporarily divided the nation, the two parts of Vietnam have become one. After three decades of isolation and civil war, Vietnam has entered the regional political scene. The ASEAN States and Vietnam have launched a major program of détente, which has already produced an atmosphere of regional friendship. During July, Vietnam's Deputy Foreign Minister Phan Hien made a goodwill visit to several of the ASEAN countries as well as to Burma and Laos. The five ASEAN countries have established diplomatic relations with Vietnam. All signs indicate that Vietnam has set out to prove to its neighbors and the world that it is determined to pursue an independent course, free from domination by either the Soviet Union or China.

These important steps toward regional amity should be welcomed by the United States. A regional organization composed of the ASEAN nations, the states of Indochina, and Burma, dedicated to peaceful intercourse, would be a significant force in maintaining stability and promoting economic progress in this volatile area. Thai officials assured me of their strong support for this concept. While endorsing a regionwide organization in principle, Burma has lingering historical suspicions.

I will describe briefly some current aspects of U.S. relations with Thailand, Burma, and Laos and then discuss the drug situation, a problem of particular concern to this Nation, as it involves Burma and Thailand.

THAILAND

In Thailand, Prime Minister Seni Pramot presides over a shaky parliamentary government. Although the ruling coalition is composed of only 4 parties, compared with 17 in the previous government led by his brother, Kukrit Pramot, there is serious dissension with the coalition. In addition, there is the ever-present threat of a military coup. While I was in the country, a crisis arose as a result of the surreptitious return to Bangkok from Taiwan of the former military strongman, Field Marshal Praphas Charasathien, who was exiled when the military government was ousted in 1973. It was widely assumed that his return was designed to stimulate overthrow of the civilian government by the military. The government's handling of the affair aroused strong passions on both the left and the right. Although Praphas was forced to leave the country, the incident has probably given encouragement both to opposition elements within the government and to antidemocratic elements in the Military Establishment.

It is said that the military, much of which is opposed to Thailand's commitment to regional détente with Vietnam, Laos, and Cambodia, is convinced that the country's experiment with democracy will fail. Although it is making a valiant attempt to survive, the future of Thailand's fledgling democratic system is less than assured. On the other hand, prospects for survival of parliamentary government are aided significantly by a reasonably bright economic picture and vivid public memories of the oppressive tactics of previous military governments. Insurgencies in the North and Northeast, and to a lesser extent in the South, continue but the problem appears little changed from last year. And the picture is not likely to improve as long as there is firm dedication by the Bangkok Government to bringing about real economic progress in neglected regions.

The withdrawal in July of the last regular U.S. military forces, leaving only a 250-man advisory unit, was a significant factor in creating favorable conditions for the establishment 2 weeks later of diplomatic relations between Thailand and Vietnam. Americans should not interpret the Thai demand for the withdrawal of U.S. forces as an unfriendly gesture. It should be seen for what it was, an inevitable adjustment to the new realities which both countries face in Southeast Asia.

Under the withdrawal agreement the United States will have certain aircraft transit rights at the Takli air base. The abuse of this privilege should be scrupulously avoided, lest it exacerbate the tenuous political situation in Thailand. Both military and economic assistance to Thailand continue, although nonconcessional economic aid, other than that for population contol and antidrug programs, will terminate next year. Military grant aid will end in 1977 also as a result of the general phaseout voted by the Congress. Consistent with Thailand's desire to stand on its own two feet, U.S. bilateral aid programs for population and antidrug activities should be terminated also if the responsibility for programs in these fields can be shifted to the United Nations.

The current Thai Government favors continuation of the SEATO treaty relationship with the United States. Drawn up following the 1954 Geneva Conference on Indochina as a device to stop the spread of communism in Southeast Asia, the SEATO treaty is no longer a viable multilateral security agreement. It has practical application only to Thailand. Although I strongly approve of Thailand's desire to maintain close ties to the United States, I do not believe that trying to breathe life into the SEATO treaty, a relic of the errors of past policy, is in the best interests of either country. Sound bilateral trade and economic relations are far more important to Thai-United States friendship than a lifeless scrap of paper. Undue emphasis on military matters would be an anachronism, inconsistent with the current interests of both countries. It is, however, important that America continue to demonstrate its desire for close, friendly relations with Thailand in ways that will promote regional cooperation and heal the wounds left by the recent war.

BURMA

The situation in Burma has changed little since last year. Burma continues rigorously to pursue a nonaligned course, keeping its distance from all of the major powers. Seven years ago in a report to the Senate, I wrote:

> The Burmese government continues to go its own way as it has for many years. It is neither overawed by the proximity of powerful neighbors nor overimpressed by the virtues of rapid development through large infusions of foreign aid. Burma's primary concern is the retention of its national and cultural identity and the development of an economic system preponderantly by its own efforts and along its own lines.

That analysis continues to be valid.

In July, a coup plot against President Ne Win's government, instigated by a number of low-ranking, but well-connected, army officers, was discovered. Although the attempt may signify eroding confidence in Ne Win's leadership within the army, it did not deter the President from leaving for Europe in mid-August for medical treatment. On the positive side, there are reliable reports that the event stimulated the government to take more aggressive action to cure the ills of Burma's stagnant and inefficient economy. A World Bank Consultative Group is being formed to aid in stimulating economic growth but, thus far, the United States has refused to join, seeking assurances of economic changes in advance of participation.

Insurgencies continue in Burma's remote mountainous regions but, according to observers, the government has made some progress within the last year in controlling the problem. Although the country's economy is notoriously mismanaged, it is a country rich in assets, both in natural resources and people. "No one dies of starvation in Burma," one top official put it. That says a great deal about the situation.

The United States owns some $12 million in Burmese currencies which are wasting away through inflation. My visit to Burma a year ago came several weeks after a devastating earthquake had seriously damaged or destroyed many Buddhist temples in historic Pagan. It required 5 months of prodding within the Government in Washington to get an Embassy request approved for a token gift of $10,000 of these currencies to aid in the restoration work at Pagan, approval that came long after all major nations had made even more substantial contributions. An Embassy request is now pending in the State Department for use of a modest amount of this U.S.-owned local currency to make needed improvements in Embassy staff apartments. I hope that not only will the Embassy's request be approved but also that a study be made of other appropriate ways to make effective use of the U.S.-owned holdings.

LAOS

With the approval of the Government of Laos, I flew from Bangkok to Vientiane in a small aircraft attached to the U.S. Embassy in Thailand, the first U.S. aircraft of any type allowed into Laos in more than a year. I view the Laotian Governments' approval of my flight as a gesture of good will toward the United States.

The new government has taken steps to improve relations with Thailand, although deep suspicions remain from the period when Thailand was used as a base for military operations against Laos. Agreement in principle was reached early this month to open several border crossings on the Mekong to facilitate trade between the two countries.

In the course of a long conversation with me, the Acting Foreign Minister, Khamphay Boupha, repeatedly made allegations that the United States was supporting anti-Lao elements in Thailand. I assured him that, according to the best information available to me, the United States was not engaged in any operations in Thailand directed against Laos.

The Lao Government seeks assistance from all sources, to repair the damage inflicted on its people and resources during many years of civil and international war. Acting Foreign Minister Khamphay told me that 500,000 Loatians were forced to leave their homes because of the war—a United Nations representative in Vientiane said that the number was as high as 700,000—and that 100,000 were killed and tens of thousands wounded, a terrible toll for a country of only 3 million people. Significant United Nations programs are underway to aid refugees and restore agricultural productivity.

Minister Khamphay assured me that his government "wants to maintain good relations with the United States on the basis of mutual respect for each other's independence, sovereignty, and territorial integrity." The Laotian Government, he said, had two objectives for its relations with the United States: First, to bring a halt to any support by the United States for what he termed the "reactionary traitors" working against Laos; and second, to obtain assistance for healing the wounds of the war.

As I noted above, on the basis of official information, I was able to assure the Laotian Deputy Foreign Minister that we were no longer involved in the internal affairs of Laos. It would be my hope that such would continue to the case. There would be no point at this time in the United States giving any support, directly or indirectly, to anti-Loatian elements inside or outside of that country, under any circumstances. As to foreign aid, I believe that, at an appropriate time, consideration should be given to providing relief aid through the United Nations or other international auspices, not as war reparations, but as a decent gesture to a poor country in a great need through little fault of its own.

One problem of concern to many Americans very much on my mind in traveling to Laos, was to seek cooperation in determining the fate of some 300 U.S. servicemen missing in action from aircraft which went down in Laos. When I raised this matter, Minister Khamphay said to me:

> The Lao have a long tradition of adhering to humanitarian principles. . . . The government has ordered the people throughout the country to look for crash sites and if the people find any they are to report to us and the information will be passed to the United States.

In a speech on Pacific policy on December 7, 1975, President Ford said that U.S. policy toward the new regimes in Indochina will be "determined by their conduct toward us. We are prepared to reciprocate gestures of goodwill—particularly the return of remains of Americans killed or missing in action or information about them." I hope that this cooperative gesture by the Laotian Government will produce helpful information. It might well be matched by a gesture on our part.

In this connection, it seems to me that the United States should send an ambassador to Laos, a country with which we still maintain formal diplomatic relations. The nomination of Galen Stone to be Ambassador to Laos was confirmed by the Senate nearly 15 months ago but he has yet to be sent to take up his post. Either he or a replacement should be sent to Vientiane. The present course smacks of a petty petulence.

NARCOTICS

The United States is making a major effort in Thailand and Burma, at a cost of several millions of dollars each year, to lessen the flow of narcotics to the United States from the Golden Triangle. The United Nations also operates antinarcotics programs in both countries.

After an investment of $8.5 million in equipment and advisers, plus the cost of an additional $2.6 million annually for regional U.S. Drug Enforcement Administration operations, there is little to show in Thailand for the American investment.

Although the growing of opium in Thailand has been illegal since 1959, the law is not enforced. According to experienced observers, a more fundamental problem is that a revolving door system under which arrested drug traffickers are quickly released is still the rule. Hong Kong authorities, who must cope with the flow of drugs from the Bangkok connection, are making significant progress in local antidrug programs but are critical of the Thai Government's laxity in dealing with drug traffickers. The authorities of other nations are also highly critical of the failure of the Thai Government to police its side of the border and of the corruption reputed to exist in the Thai police system.

To be sure, the Thai Government has to deal with many problems. Stopping the Bangkok drug traffic, however, is a major headache. Until there is a much greater commitment to deal with the problem, putting more millions of American money into buying helicopters, radios, jeeps, and other fancy equipment for the Thai antinarcotics police will not have the desired effect.

According to U.S. officials, Burma is making effective use of 12 helicopters the United States has provided within the last year for antinarcotics operations. Six more are yet to be delivered. The Burmese Army has begun a program of physically destroying opium poppy fields, which, according to estimates, has reduced this year's potential crop from 470 tons to 343 tons, compared with an estimated 440 tons, produced in Burma last year. It is said, optimistically perhaps, that Burma's opium production can be virtually eliminated within 3 or 4 years, if an effective herbicide eradication program is initiated and crop substitution schemes now being planned have appeal to the traditional opium growers. Efforts have been made to establish a U.S. Drug Enforcement Agency presence in Burma, a move resisted in Burma. In my judgment, the arguments against bringing DEA personnel into Burma are fully tenable and there is no reasonable justification for such an expansion of the bureaucracy.

Laos is not a factor in the external opium trade, according to most experts. The current Lao Government is taking drastic measures to cure drug addicts, sending them to an island in the middle of the Mekong for intensive treatment. As to China, all U.S. officials within the area agree that it is not a source of narcotics for the outside world, producing only as much opium as is required for internal medical needs.

In my report last year, I expressed concern over involvement by U.S. narcotics operatives in police actions abroad. As a result, Congress adopted a proposal which prohibits any U.S. personnel abroad from participating in any foreign police arrest actions in connection with narcotics operations. The Drug Enforcement Administration has issued guidelines for implementation of this provision and I have been assured by Mr. Peter Bensinger, the DEA Administrator, that both the letter and the spirit of the law will be strictly enforced.

In view of the fact that the drug problem is international in scope, I also recommended last year that the United States channel assistance to other countries for antinarcotics efforts through the United Nations. Congress has directed the President to make a study of how to achieve this objective. In both Thailand and Burma, for example, the United Nations already conducts crop substitution and other anti-drug programs. Burma, intent on maintaining its distance from all major powers, has indicated keen interest in obtaining through the United Nations assistance of the kind we now provide on a bilateral basis. I believe that leaders of the Thai Government would also be more comfortable if the United Nations took the lead from the United States in this field.

The Committee on Foreign Relations should make a thorough study of the foreign operations of the antinarcotics program. It is an expensive program, costing $37.5 million for direct aid alone in the last fiscal year. It is also an administrative nightmare involving the operations abroad of at least five Departments and agencies—the DEA, AID, CIA, the Department of Agriculture, and the Department of State, which, through our ambassadors, is supposed to be in charge of the entire operation. Pending submission of the Presidential report on shifting emphasis to the United Nations or regional programs, the committee should make a careful study of the management and cost effectiveness of all current drug operations abroad.

NONALIGNED CONFERENCE

While I was in Southeast Asia, an event of significance took place in Sri Lanka, the Fifth Conference of the Non-Aligned Nations. The delegates at Colombo represented two-thirds of the nations of the world and one-third of its inhabitants, a three-fold increase from the 28 nations represented at the founding meeting at Bandung two decades ago. Much of the rhetoric that came out of the conference hall in Colombo was not very palatable to us. Nevertheless, it is in our national interest to pay close attention to the Third World, to what the leaders of these countries think and seek. The United States is rapidly becoming a have-not Nation in regard to basic resources on which we and other industrial nations are dependent. The Third World straddles a good share of the world's supply of these resources and can no longer be ignored.

I returned from my visit to Southeast Asia with a firm conviction that, in general, developments in the region are moving in the right direction, both for the nations concerned and for the United States. The Southeast Asian countries appear determined to pursue an independent path, free of outside domination by any power. There are encouraging signs that, on a parallel tract, most also seek to further regional understanding, or, at a minimum, to join hands in preventing undue interference from outsiders.

Vietnam, contrary to many predictions, is demonstrating a desire to live in peace with its neighbors. It has now applied for membership in the United Nations. I hope that the United States will not again veto its application. Our relations with the nations of Indochina should be shaped to fit reality. The reality is that new governments are in firm control in Vietnam, Cambodia, and Laos.

Seven years ago the Senate approved a resolution, offered by Senator Cranston, which stated that—

When the United States recognizes a foreign government and exchanges representatives with it, this does not of itself imply that the United States approves of the form, ideology, or policy of that government.

In other words, the Senate has said that diplomatic recognition is simply a recognition of de facto and de jure control. That should be the basis for U.S. policy toward the new governments of Indochina.

Americans are a generous people, willing to bury the mistakes of the past and look to the future. A generation ago our Nation was locked in a life and death struggle with Germany and Japan. Today they are allied with us. National interests are not immutable. Interests, and the policies to further them, must reflect a changing world. We should look to the past for wisdom, to learn how to shape the future, not for the purpose of perpetuating animosity or bitterness.

I urge the next President to make a thorough review of U.S. policy in Asia with a view to wiping the slate clean. It is not easy for bureaucracies or individuals to shake off the habits or associations of decades. Much of the Government foreign affairs bureacracy, from State Department policymakers to CIA operatives, appear to me to be still too closely attuned to policies of the past.

There are deep suspicions in the region that remnants of operations related to the old policies continue, particularly as to CIA operations. It may be that intelligence gathering, for example, has not yet been keyed to the new situation in Indochina and to the goal of normalizing relations with China. In any event, I hope that the Select Committee on Intelligence will make a thorough review of current intelligence operations in Asia to insure that they are consistent in all respects with long-range national objectives.

In closing, I add a short postscript to my recent report to the Committee on Foreign Relations concerning Japan and Korea.

Both en route to and on return from Southeast Asia, I stopped in Tokyo to receive a briefing on recent developments from officers of the U.S. Embassy. The Lockheed scandal continues to dominate Japanese political affairs as the Watergate affair did here for so long. Prime Minister Miki's determination to bring out all the facts, regardless of where the chips might fall, has created great controversy within his own party but has met with widespread public and news media approval. It is to be hoped that the matter will be handled in such a way that neither the confidence of the Japanese people in their governmental processes nor that nation's political stability will be damaged.

As to the incident in Korea, the brutal killing of two American officers in the joint security area of the Korean demilitarized zone, and subsequent actions have aroused passions on both sides, underlining what I said in my report scarcely a month ago: "Korea is a time bomb which has yet to be defused."

This is not the first inflammatory incident to occur in the nearly quarter of a century since the cease-fire agreement that ended the Korean war. And it will not be the last. When fighting men are placed in close proximity to the enemy on a daily basis incidents are bound to happen. It takes only a match to start a conflagration.

The President is to be commended for having insisted that U.S. officials keep cool in the recent tragedy because under existing circumstances U.S. forces will be involved inevitably in any outbreak of fighting in Korea. The swift dispatch to Korea of additional U.S. attack aircraft and a carrier task force demonstrate that under current contingency plans, U.S. military forces will be involved from the outset in any resumption of hostilities, despite the constitutional responsibility of Congress to declare war.

The United States is in a vise in Korea from which it must eventually extricate itself by a phased withdrawal of forces while simultaneously seeking a permanent solution to the conflict. It is to be hoped that the recent incident will not delay U.S. initiatives in that direction.

Exhibit 1

EXCERPTS FROM WINDS OF CHANGE—EVOLVING RELATIONS AND
INTERESTS IN SOUTHEAST ASIA—AUGUST, 1975

I. THREE VARIATIONS ON NEUTRALISM

President Nixon's visit to Peking in 1972 released strong winds of
change in the international relationships of Asia. The collapse in
South Vietnam and Cambodia intensified these currents. Visible
changes already include the restoration of contact between the
United States and China looking in the direction of normalcy after
many years of acrimonious confrontation. This shift has been a key
factor in enabling us to reduce the U.S. military presence in Asia
from some 650,000 at the height of the Indochina war to less than
60,000 at present. Moreover, a further reduction will take place in
the months ahead as U.S. forces are withdrawn from Thailand.

U.S. policy, in short, is beginning to reflect the fact that the United
States is a Pacific nation, but not a power on the Asian mainland.
The waters of the Pacific touch the shores of the United States on
the West Coast, at Hawaii, Alaska, the territory of Guam and the
U.S. trust territories. They also beat against the coastlines of seven
nations to which we have made security commitments—Japan,
South Korea, Taiwan, the Philippines, Thailand, Australia and New
Zealand—as well as the shores of the Soviet Union and China. What
takes place in this vast region is of deep concern to this nation.
However, concern and capacity to influence are quite different. What
we began to perceive in Korea and saw very clearly in Indochina
is that our capacity to influence the flow of history on the Asian
Mainland itself is quite limited on the basis of any rational input of
manpower and resources.

After the birth of the People's Republic of China in 1949, we established a policy of containment of Communist China. It was a
policy which sought to line up nations on an either "for or against"
basis with "neutralism" regarded as something to be spurned. A
ring of treaties was engineered in an effort to use U.S. power and influence to choke off what were held to be China's aggressive designs
on its neighbors. In Southeast Asia, both Thailand and the Philippines
linked their foreign policy directly to what became a U.S. crusade
against communism on the Asia Mainland, Burma and Cambodia,
each in its own way, tried to walk the tight rope of non-involvement.
The former did so throughout the Indochina war, in part, by rejecting
U.S. and other forms of foreign aid. Under Prince Norodom Sihanouk,
Cambodia also held the line of non-involvement successfully for
many years. When the Prince was overthrown by a military coup,
however, the Khmers paid the cost in five years of bloody war.

The overthrow of Sihanouk also added more U.S. casualties and billions to U.S. costs in Indochina as this nation went from non-involvement to the aid of the successor military regime in Phnom Penh.

Throughout Southeast Asia, nations are now making major reassessments of their relationships. Nationalism and neutrality, mixed with a budding interest in regional cooperation, are the driving forces at work. Neutralism takes on different characteristics in each of the Southeast Asian nations. Burma is a study of traditional neutrality with a heavy accent on isolationism. Thailand, the only nation in the region to remain free of colonial rule before World War II, is engaged in writing another chapter in its long history of seeking to balance its independence amidst shifting political currents. Three decades after close alignment with and vestigial dependency on the United States, the Republic of the Philippines is moving into the more open waters of international relations and accelerating its efforts to achieve a fully independent identity.

As new relationships evolve in Southeast Asia, new problems are emerging among the nations in the area and in their relations with the United States. Changes in an old order always carry a degree of painful adjustment. It is to be hoped, however, that out of the old, eventually will emerge a new spirit of self-reliance and regional cooperation. In that fashion, the independent nations of the region may be able to live together in a zone of peace respected by all of the great powers. That is the goal towards which each nation visited, in its own way and to some degree, all of them together, seemed to be moving.

The Asian nations are very likely to call for adjustments of all of the relationships with the West which grew out of a previous state of dependency. We should do our best in our own interests to accommodate to changes of this kind. They involve, in many cases, as in Indochina, the lightening of an excessive and one-sided burden which has been maintained for decades by the people of the United States. From our own point of view, it would be desirable to subject the Southeast Asia Collective Defense Treaty, the so-called Manila Pact, to critical reexamination. The treaty seems to me of little relevance to the security of this Nation in the contemporary situation. In fact, it may be more a liability than an asset to all of the signatories. As for our relations with Indochina, it would seem to me helpful in dealing with the vestigial problems of the war and in paving the way for a peaceful future to establish direct contact with the successor governments in Vietnam and Cambodia at an appropriate time.

It would be unfortunate if out of indignation or disillusionment we should turn our backs on Asia. More in line with our interests would be to seek to understand more clearly what is transpiring on that continent. Our young people, in particular, need as much exposure as possible to the changes in Asia since they will experience in the years ahead most of the consequences. Through diplomacy and cultural contacts we should be able to harmonize our reasonable national interests in security, trade and cultural cross fertilization with the emerging situation in Southeast Asia. The present transition need not be a source of anxiety if it is approached in that fashion. Indeed, we could be on the verge of a new era which could bring great benefits both to the Asian countries and to this Nation.

II. BURMA

Neutrality and nonalignment

Under President Ne Win, Burma has navigated a course of neutralism and nonalignment for many years. Its relations with the great neighboring states of China and India are correct and formal and the same is true for the Soviet Union and the United States. Burma has no intimates and seeks none. It has sought to avoid foreign entanglements. Although it was an early member of the United Nations, only in 1973 did the nation even join the World Bank and the Asian Development Bank. In the United Nations and other international forums, Burma has abstained on many divisive issues. For years it has recognized both Koreas and both Vietnams.

Burma was an observer of what happened to the Indochinese nations when they were drawn into great power rivalries. Their tragic experience was such as to provide proof to the Burmese Government of the correctness of its own policy. Whatever its shortcomings, this policy has served to keep Burma out of the conflicts which have beset others in Southeast Asia. Furthermore, isolated by natural mountain barriers on the east, west, and north the Burmans have been able to preserve to a greater degree than most nations in the region, their traditional culture.

Speculation in Burma is to the effect that its doors may soon open wider, evidencing, some say, a change in attitude towards the outside world. One Burmese official observed to me, however, that what has happened is "not that Burma has changed but that the world has changed." He went on to explain that a U.S. policy of détente with the Soviet Union and the new U.S. relationship with China significantly altered the framework of Burma's neutralism and made foreign contacts, notably with the United States, more feasible.

Foreign observers, when discussing Burma's economy, generally describe it as "stagnant" or "sick." While it is obvious to a visitor that there is a great deal of poverty, the usual economic yardsticks are not exact or even very relevant when applied to a rice-based agrarian society. The extremes of poor and rich, for example, are not seen in Burma as in many other countries. Burma's economy is not rocketing ahead but neither as in Indochina has the land been devastated and hundreds of thousands killed and maimed by warfare. Also avoided so far have been the cultural upheavals and environmental despoliation which are often associated with economic development via heavy influxes of outside capital and foreign aid.

Nevertheless, there are manifestations of political dissatisfaction from time to time which center in Rangoon and are probably directed in part, at least, at the lack of economic progress and opportunity. Three major anti-government demonstrations by workers and students have occurred during the last year and a half. Colleges and universities have been closed from time to time and leaders of workers demonstrations have been sentenced to long prison terms.

Although a new Burmese Constitution was adopted last year, the government remains based on army leadership. Sixteen of 18 cabinet officers are military or ex-military men. While farming is still on a private basis, as are many shops and stores, the government runs much of the rest of the economy. Staples, such as rice, oil, and cloth are rationed, with scanty allotments. This system, plus a shortage of consumer goods generally undergirds a so-called "shadow economy" or black market. Although stable until the last year or so, prices are now rising. Rice stocks available for export, the country's principal source of foreign exchange, are dwindling due to lack of substantial increases in output coupled with population growth. In the last thirty years, the population has almost doubled to 30 million. The government is considering new incentives to raise rice production and recently increased the price paid to the farmer by 30 percent. As yet, however, policies have not been devised to surmount the dilemma of a dwindling per capita food supply as against what is seen as a possible loss of security and national identity which might be occasioned by limiting population growth in the midst of towering neighbors.

One way to help alleviate this dilemma, at least for the immediate future, would be by the discovery of petroleum in exportable quantities. After years of rejecting private investment, last year, Burma leased offshore tracts to two American oil companies, Exxon and Cities Service, and two companies from other countries. While the drilling has not yet yielded results, the Burmese believe the prospects are good. Burma is also seeking by its own efforts to extend present onshore oil fields which supply 70 percent of the nation's modest current needs. The government has not shown any interest in foreign involvement in the exploration for minerals, with which according to technical reports, Burma is generously endowed.

A part of Burma's imports are presently being financed by loans from the World Bank and the Asian Development Bank and by bilateral agreements with West Germany and Japan. Three small Asian Development Bank projects are now underway. While the U.S. has not provided new dollar assistance to Burma since 1963, a consortium arrangement under the World Bank and the International Monetary Fund which involve foreign aid contributions by the United States, Japan, and Western European countries is under consideration.

The Burmese are in the process of repairing the severe damage caused by an earthquake in early July at Pagan, an area of historical significance and the site of numerous edifices and shrines dating from the 11th Century. They are hampered by lack of funds which are being raised through public subscription. Various nations have made contributions through their embassies in Rangoon for this very worthwhile endeavor. Shortly before I arrived, U.S. Embassy officials had asked Washington for permission to make a small monetary contribution to assist in the repair of the damage at Pagan. The request was denied, apparently on some semantic or obscure basis and the matter was buffeted from pillar to post in the bureaucracy. It is amazing to find that in an Executive Branch which frequently finds ways unknown even to the Congress to rush tens of millions in aid to shore up a sinking regime as in the closing days of the Cambodian debacle, is unable to find a basis for a modest human gesture in the face of a natural disaster such as occurred in Burma last summer. One can only note that if more authority is necessary to act in a situation such as this, why has it not long since been requested?

The drug trade and insurgents along the Burmese border create a dangerous mixture. Twenty groups, most of them based on ethnic divisions and some quite small and of little contemporary significance, are now in various degrees of insurrection or insurbordination with regard to the government in Rangoon. It is possible to divide the factions into three basic groupings. The first type seeks to replace the existing government and is exemplified by the Burma Communist Party, the largest single dissident element. Typified by the Kachin Independence Army (KIA), a second group seeks autonomy in ethnic areas. The third consists simply of out-and-out drug traffickers and bandits, some of whom are remnants or descendants of the forces associated with the National Government which fled from China in 1949 and which, for a time, were supported from Taiwan.

Opium is a traditional crop in the hill areas of Northeast Burma. It is estimated that the crop may reach 440 metric tons this year even though the price is currently depressed because of the loss of the South Vietnamese market. All the insurgent groups are believed to be financed, at least in part, through the drug traffic. The Chinese (Nationalist) Irregular Force which is still organized into the 3rd and 5th divisions is the most important group involved in the drug traffic. Another element is the Shan United Army, which operates in the Northern Shan states.

Each organization has its own "turf" in the remote and scarcely accessible border areas as well as its own methods of operations. In simplified form, the cycle of operations, runs as follows: the trafficker buys the crude opium from the grower, transports it to the Thai border, sells it, uses the proceeds to buy arms or other goods, brings the arms and goods back into Burma, sells them on the black market. The cycle is completed when the proceeds from the black market sales are used to buy more opium.

The Burmese Government is concerned with the drug traffic both because of the growing consumption of drugs in the country and because suppression of the trade is seen as an essential element in dealing effectively with the insurgency problem. After an initial reluctance, Burma has agreed to accept eighteen helicopters which are available under the U.S. narcotics control program. Four helicopters have been delivered, on a trial basis, and, if results are mutually satisfactory, the remainder will be turned over, in due course, to the Burmese government.

In addition to this arrangement, there have been some small Burmese purchases of U.S. military related goods. The Burmese government, however, has indicated no interest in renewal of military aid program or in obtaining military training for its forces in the United States.

A note of caution is indicated in regard to cooperation in drug suppression. The zeal of U.S. enforcement officials in trying to get at the sources of drugs is understandable and merits much applause. Nevertheless, there are other questions involved in Burmese-U.S. relations. For too long in the administration of U.S. policies, we have tended to assume responsibility for problems which are more properly those of other nations or of the international community. One form of involvement in the internal affairs of other nations can lead very rapidly to other forms, as the bitter Indochina experience should have taught us.

In my judgment, therefore, any further U.S. assistance to foreign countries for their internal use in anti-drug problems, if warranted at all, would seem more appropriately to be funneled through international bodies. Whatever funds Congress thinks justified for this activity might well go as a contribution to the U.N.'s Narcotics Control program. Moreover, any activity of U.S. narcotics agents in Burma or any other nation in Southeast Asia, for that matter, must remain under the strict supervision and firm control of the U.S. Ambassador who is in the best position to know what practices are or are not possible in the light of our total relationship with the country concerned.

After my visit to Burma six years ago, I wrote: "The Burmese government continues to go its own way as it has for many years. It is neither overawed by the proximity of powerful neighbors nor over-impressed by the virtues of rapid development through large infusions of foreign aid. Burma's primary concern is the retention of its national and cultural identity and the development of an economic system preponderantly by its own efforts and along its own lines."

These are still the major pre-occupations of the Ne Win government. The nation has succeeded in maintaining its national and cultural identity. Its economic situation, however, is still very tenuous.

As for our relations with Burma, while some strengthening of cultural and technical exchange either on a bilateral or multilateral basis may be desirable and possible, my view is that we would be well-advised to avoid scrupulously any inclinations towards a deepening involvement in Burmese affairs. Such inclinations would not be welcomed in Burma as in its best interests. Clearly, too, they would not be in the best interest of this nation.

III. THAILAND

After four decades of military rule, Thailand is attempting anew to forge a democratic system. At the same time, there is underway a major revision in foreign relationships. Following student uprisings, in October 1973, the military government of Field Marshal Thanom Kittikachorn was ousted and Thanom and other government leaders fled the country. This development, coupled with the rapidly changing situation in Asia, initiated by President Nixon's trip to Peking, and culminating in the collapse in Indochina, has brought about a sweeping reappraisal by Thailand of its foreign policy.

Until the fall of the Thanom government, Thailand had maintained a close relationship—some termed it a "client-state" relationship—with the United States. Now that has changed, with Thailand moving away from the long intimacy with the United States and, at the same time, seeking better relations with its neighbors in Indochina and Asia. How this land of 44 million people handles the turn towards political democracy and a new foreign policy will have far-reaching consequences for the over-all relationships in and around the Asian continent.

Political and economic situation

Prime Minister Khukrit Pramot, leader of the Social Action Party, has governed Thailand since mid-March with a coalition of eight parties. His own party, with only 18 seats, is a distant third in terms of party strength in the Parliament. While the Thai King, Phumiphon Adunyadet, serves primarily as the symbol of national unity, the monarchy is still a factor in state affairs, particularly, in times of crisis. The present Thai political system is based on a Parliament consisting of 269 seats in an elected Lower House and a 100-member appointed Upper House. Elections earlier this year attracted 42 parties and 2,191 candidates. Predictably, the results were inconclusive. There are now representatives from 23 parties sitting in the Parliament which, when I visited it, was meeting in a joint session and engaged in spirited debate over an aspect of ASEAN. Despite earlier predictions of a short and unhappy life, the Parliamentary structure is managing to hold together and is serving as a vehicle for operative government.

The Khukrit cabinet, apart from the difficulties inherent in any coalition and, especially in one emerging from the trauma of an abrupt shift from military authoritarianism, is subject to three basic pressures; a volatile student movement; long-standing insurgencies in the north the northeast and the south; and the ever present possibility of a military coup.

The student movement wields influence, as is often the case in Asian nations, far beyond numbers. There is a working relationship between the students and labor on most issues and this coalition constitutes the most potent force in current Thai politics. It may be less of a factor, however, than it was two years ago at the time of the ousting of the dictatorship. Public reaction in Bangkok to past excesses, it is said, has caused student leaders to be more discriminating in choosing issues on which to exert their pressure.

One personal incident was instructive. When I arrived for an appointment with the Prime Minister, hundreds of out of work Thai guards at U.S. military bases, who are being discharged as the bases are phased out, were engaged in a demonstration demanding final pay adjustments. The guards were not on U.S. payrolls but, rather, were paid indirectly on the basis of U.S. contracts with Thai military leaders of the previous regime, some of whom apparently have fled the country. Since the demonstration was taking place in front of the Prime Minister's offices, it was necessary to postpone the meeting lest the presence of a visiting American official trigger more serious difficulties.

Ever present in the background of Thai politics is the potential for a military coup. While the government appears to command the loyalty of the armed forces, rumors of possible coups abound in Bangkok. Perhaps, the principal deterrent is the public revulsion with the rampant corruption of the previous military regime and the possibility that a coup at this time would again bring on a militant student-labor reaction.

The role of the military has been deemphasized by the present government which appears to want to direct its energies towards social and economic needs. Heretofore much of the government's interest centered on Bangkok. With 4 million people, Bangkok is Thailand's only major city and it is scarcely representative of the nation. The gap between Bangkok and the rest of the country is great. Per capita income in the capital, for example, is $600 per year, but it is only about $200 nationally, and it is, perhaps, not more than $75 per year in the most troublesome insurgent area, the northeast. There has been little spread of commerce and industry from Bangkok to the countryside. The city, in some respects, is like a foreign land to

most Thais. Its traffic jams, westernized practices and political maneu-
vering are quite alien to the villagers who make up the vast majority
of the country's population.

Neglect of the villages is a major factor in fueling the insurgency
movements. In the north the insurgents are ethnic groups often
involved in the drug traffic. In the northeast, the problem is peasant
discontent and Thai against Thai. In the south, it is largely Malay
muslim or Chinese against Thais.

Over the years, there have been any number of anti-insurgency
campaigns launched by Bangkok, all liberally financed with U.S.
funds and, often, abetted with advice from various U.S. agencies.
None has brought any appreciable results. The insurgent movements
have continued to grow, with a total of perhaps 8,500 now under
arms in the northeast alone. The Khukrit government seems to be
aware that the problem cannot be solved unless there is more effective
contact between a heretofore remote government in Bangkok and the
people in the localities. It is trying new approaches which include a
form of revenue sharing to channel funds to the poorest areas. Also
recognized is the need to change the attitudes of the underpaid and
corrupt bureaucracy in the insurgent areas. While it may be difficult
to persuade soldiers and police who have reaped much of the financial
benefit of past anti-insurgent campaigns to become benefactors of
villagers, at least an effort is being made to bring about a reorienta-
tion. The government's five year plan also emphasizes economic
growth in the rural areas and reduction in income disparities. It
remains to be seen whether the benefits will actually reach the people.

The Thai economy has weathered the oil crisis, the world recession,
and the phase-out of U.S. military involvement in Indochina. Although
the rate of inflation was 60 percent in 1974, up from an average of 4
percent in the years before, it has been falling and will probably be
down to about 10 percent for 1975. Increased earnings from agricultural exports have been a prime factor in countering oil price increases.
The impact of both the recession and the uncertainty over political
developments in the region have been felt in the slackening of foreign
investment. Tourism, too, is down. Nevertheless, Thailand enjoyed a
$400 million surplus in its over-all balance of payments in 1974 in
the face of a deficit of $657 million in trade. The difference was made
up by foreign aid, oil concession payments, tourism and capital
inflows.

The United States has given Thailand large amounts of economic
aid over the years, much of it in the last decade for the so-called
counter-insurgency programs. Thus far, a total of $672 million in
economic aid has been provided by the United States. For fiscal
year 1976, $12 million has been requested.

In an economy as formidable as Thailand's, $12 million must be
regarded as relatively inconsequential. The government's political
and economic policies are the critical factors in shaping the nation's
future. There would appear, therefore, to be little relevance to either
country in the continuance of the bilateral aid program. Indeed, the
time seems very propitious to end this vestige of "clientism" and to
place the relationship of the two nations on a firm plane of mutual
respect, with accent on mutually beneficial exchange.

Petroleum

There are prospects for major offshore petroleum strikes in the Gulf of Siam on Thailand's east coast and in the Andaman Sea west of the Kra Isthmus. Twenty-five wells have been drilled by American companies in the Gulf of Siam. Oil has been found, but the potential is not yet ascertainable. There could be international difficulties in some areas since most Thai concessions, overlap in part, territory also claimed by Cambodia. Thus far, however, there has not been any drilling in disputed areas. Some concessions have also been issued for the Andaman Sea but work there is not likely to start until next year. Thailand has already received more than $75 million for drilling rights from foreign prospectors. Renewed consideration is also being given by the Thai government to a proposal to join with Japan in constructing a major pipeline stretching across the Kra Isthmus, and terminating in a large refinery which would refine Persian Gulf crude for shipment to Japan.

Drugs

Thailand is a major site in the international drug problem, not so much as a producer but as the route of transshipment of opium brought in from elsewhere in Southeast Asia. Estimates indicate that about 40–45 tons of opium per year are actually produced in Thailand. This level is sufficient only to meet local demand.

Although some Thai officials may still be parties to the drug trade, the level of involvement is reported to be much lower than in the past. Contrary to the situation in Burma, drugs do not seem to be a significant source of financial support for insurgents but, rather, a means for personal or syndicate enrichment.

Thailand receives equipment from the United States under the narcotics control program. In fiscal year 1975, $4.8 million was provided, with $3.7 million more programmed for FY 1976. Bangkok is a regional headquarters for the U.S. Drug Enforcement Agency (DEA) which is active throughout Southeast Asia. The agency has a regional budget of $500,000, but the figure does not include assistance to other governments which runs into the millions. There are 26 U.S. agents in Thailand and they are involved in operational actions as well as intelligence gathering. The day before my arrival, for example, U.S. agents and Thai police had carried out a joint raid on an opium refinery.

This sort of U.S. anti-drug activities in Thailand seems to be highly dubious. Quite apart from the expenditure of U.S. funds, the direct participation by U.S. agents in police activities within Thailand amounts to involvement in internal Thai affairs. While it undoubtedly is meritorious in objective, it is a foot-in-the-door, a point of entry which could lead to extensions and in the end, renewed entrapment in the internal affairs of that nation at renewed cost to the people of the United States. The sorry history of military and economic aid and other activity in Indochina and Thailand over the past two decades should serve as a precaution in this respect. Police actions, including local drug enforcement, are functions of indigenous governments. If there is a U.S. role it should be limited to the exchange of information and intelligence with appropriate Thai or other officials. Beyond that point, U.S. financial assistance for antidrug operations at whatever level may be set by the Congress, in my judgment, is best channeled through international or regional organizations.

Foreign policy and U.S.-Thai relations

President Nixon's trip to Peking and the end of U.S. involvement in Indochina have created a new milieu for Thai foreign policy. From direct links and intimate cooperation with the United States in matters of security, Thailand has moved towards a neutral position. An effort is now being made by Bangkok to assure good relations with all the major powers. A case in point was Prime Minister Khukrit's visit to Peking in July which resulted in the establishment of diplomatic relations with China. So, too, was the official protest to the United States over the use of Thai bases in the Mayaguez affair. That incident, moreover, was followed by a demand for the complete withdrawal of U.S. forces from Thailand.

The outcome of the Indochina war was not only a factor in the new Thai approach to China, it also resulted in intensified interest in closer association with the Southeast Asian nations. Within five months after taking office, Khukrit visited not only Peking but all of the ASEAN countries. Thailand joined in support of the proposal to create in Southeast Asia a zone of "peace, freedom, and neutrality" which would be guaranteed by the great powers. There is no indication thus far, however, that this grouping will include any type of joint security arrangement. In that sense it would not be a substitute for the SEATO Organization which Prime Minister Khukrit and President Ferdinand Marcos of the Philippines have urged should be "phased out to make it accord with new realities in the region." This proposal, it should be noted, relates only to the organized activities under the Southeast Asian Treaty and the large headquarters staff in Bangkok. It does not involve a renunciation of the actual treaty, the so-called Manila Pact. Thailand is the only signatory in the area, however, to which the Pact now has practical application insofar as a U.S. security commitment is concerned. Pakistan renounced the treaty several years ago and the Philippines, Australia, and New Zealand, are tied to the United States by other defense arrangements.

The security relationship between the United States and Thailand is complicated by the existence of the 1962 Rusk-Thanat communique in which the obligations of the Manila Pact were held to be both joint and several. Under that interpretation, it would seem the multilateral SEATO treaty would also amount to a bilateral U.S.-Thai treaty. Thus, the treaty, potentially, has far more significance than the "scrap of paper," as it is often called today. An attack for example, by an enemy in Southeast Asia could conceivably lead on a Thai call on the United States to come to its aid notwithstanding the disinclination of any other of the signatories to do so.

The fact is that the Manila Pact was born of an old and now altered view of China. It is of no current relevance to U.S. interests in Asia. Left in abeyance it is, perhaps, a source of potential mischief or embarrassment. We would be well-advised, therefore, to reexamine this agreement forthwith, with a view to its termination.

It should be noted in this connection that Prime Minister Khukrit has called for the complete withdrawal of the 19,000 U.S. military forces in Thailand by the end of March 1976. Some references, however, have been made to the possible retention of a standby capacity at the U Taphao Base, manned by a small caretaker force.

For more than a decade, my view has been that the United States in its own interests should withdraw militarily from the Southeast Asian mainland, "lock, stock and barrel." It remains my judgment that it is not in the interest of this nation, nor probably, in the interest of Thailand to have a U.S. capacity retained at any of the installations in Thailand. There should be no toe-hold which would serve as a potential source of reinvolvement of U.S. military forces on the Southeast Asian Mainland.

LAOS—THE SANDS RUN OUT

It has been said that in Laos the French laid foundations of sand and that we tried to build on them. As seen from Thailand, the sands have run out. Since the fall of Cambodia and South Vietnam, the Pathet Lao have rapidly expanded their control of Laos. The advance occurred without much resistance or bloodshed, with the opposition tending to evaporate or flee the country. Three of the five government military commanders had left the country by early August and another left shortly afterwards.

In the capital of Vientiane, the Pathet Lao have also extended their control of the coalition central government. Prime Minister Souvanna Phouma is still in nominal command but he is reported to be virtually powerless. The King remains on the throne but is said not to play a political role. Laos is now described as a "Democratic People's Kingdom."

U.S. relations with Laos are strained and minimal following the forced closing of U.S. aid operations last June. The size of the U.S. mission dropped from 800 (including dependents) in April 1975 to 32 by mid-August. It is estimated that there are also some 50 other Americans without official status remaining in Laos. U.S. assistance is not being provided to Laos as a result of a prohibition contained in the continuing appropriations resolution for FY 1976. The new U.S. Ambassador to Laos has been confirmed by the Senate, but as of late-summer had not yet been ordered to his post. In this fashion, a U.S. involvement of 22 years which cost billions of dollars and many lives, is drawing to a close.

Exactly 20 years ago, in 1955, on the occasion of a third visit to Laos, I reported to the Committee as follows:

"* * * military aid policies which seek to do more than bulwark the security forces to the point where they can cope with armed minorities and stop occasional border sallies seem to me to be highly unrealistic. By the same token economic aid programs which attempt to move an ancient pastoral country overnight from the age of the oxcart to that of the airplane are equally unsound to say the least. Both, in attempting to do too much, in my opinion, can do incalculable harm.

"In Laos as in Cambodia, there has been an enormous increase in United States activity and in the size of the (U.S. official) mission during the past year. At the time of my first visit to Vientiane in 1953, there were two Americans in the entire country. Now (1955) there are some 45. Accordingly, I recommend that the Executive Branch, as in the case of Cambodia, review the extent of our activity in Laos and the size of the mission with a view to keeping both within the realm of the reasonable."

CHARTING A NEW COURSE

Southeast Asia in a
Time of Change

LETTER OF TRANSMITTAL

DECEMBER 10, 1976.

Hon. JOHN SPARKMAN,
Chairman, Committee on Foreign Relations,
U.S. Senate, Washington, D.C.

DEAR MR. CHAIRMAN: Transmitted herewith is a report of my final official mission abroad as a United States Senator. It contains observations which result from a series of visits this year to various parts of Asia and the Pacific.

During July I spent eight days in Japan following which I sent Mr. Francis R. Valeo and Mr. Norvill Jones, who accompanied me, to Korea and Taiwan, respectively, to obtain current information concerning issues relating to those countries. A report of that study, "The End of the Postwar Era: Time for a New Partnership of Equality With Japan", was filed with the Committee and is included as an appendix to this report. In August, I traveled to Thailand, Laos, and Burma to view the situation in that part of Southeast Asia. My observations as a result of that visit were reported to the Senate in a speech on August 26, which is also included as an appendix to this report.

The third segment of my travels to assess the current scene in Asia was to the People's Republic of China where I spent three weeks during September and October. My observations on China were transmitted to the Committee on November 18. After leaving China, I visited the Philippines, Indonesia, and Papau New Guinea.

In the Philippines I met with President Ferdinand E. Marcos and officials of the Ministry of Foreign Affairs; in Indonesia I conferred with President Suharto, leaders of Parliament, and met informally with other government officials; and in Papau New Guinea I had informative talks with Acting Prime Minister Sir Maori Kiki and also had opportunity for discussions with other local officials. In each country I also received briefings from the staff of the local U.S. Mission. While in Indonesia, I received a briefing on developments in both Malaysia and Singapore from officers of the United States Embassy in each country who met with me in Jakarta for that purpose.

This report contains both observations on the non-China portion of my last mission and some observations on the general situation in Asia.

I was accompanied on the trip by Senator John Glenn and his wife, Anna, both of whom contributed greatly to the mission. I wish to express my appreciation to the Department of State and to the U.S. missions in each country visited; the Department of the Air Force for transportation; Deputy Assistant Secretary of State Victor Dikeos for his efficient handling of logistics and other details, my assistant Mrs. Salpee Sahagian and Senator Glenn's secretary, Miss Kathy Prosser, for their able and willing help at all times; Dr. Thomas Lowe of the Navy Medical Corps for his services; Mr. Francis R. Valeo, Secretary of the Senate, Mr. Charles R. Gellner, Senior specialist in Foreign Affairs of the Congressional Research Service, Library of Congress, and Mr. Norvill Jones of the staff of the Committee on Foreign Relations, for their assistance.

I also wish to express special appreciation to my wife, Maureen, for her usual valuable contribution.

Sincerely,

MIKE MANSFIELD.

CHARTING A NEW COURSE: SOUTHEAST ASIA IN A TIME OF CHANGE

I. Introduction

Since President Nixon's visit to Peking in 1972 winds of change have swept Asia. It is in Southeast Asia that those winds have blown the strongest, increasing in intensity as a result of the 1975 collapse of the U.S.-supported governments in Indochina. Nations in the region are making major reassessments of their relationships. Nationalism, neutrality, and a growing interest in regional cooperation are the significant factors at work. The Association of Southeast Asian Nations (ASEAN), formed in 1970 by Indonesia, Malaysia, Thailand, the Philippines, and Singapore, has been the principal vehicle for advancing regional cooperation. Two underlying principles have contributed to ASEAN's success to date, a common readiness to refrain from trying to force agreement on contentious issues and a policy of avoiding becoming identified with any major power. Gradualism and a recognition that the interests of member states differ have governed the group's cautious approach. As an organization its goal is not to become a super-state but something of a club to promote common interests.

In April 1976 the heads of state of the ASEAN nations, meeting on the Indonesian island of Bali in the organization's first summit meeting, signed a Treaty of Amity and Cooperation which, among other things, created a mechanism for settling regional disputes. At this meeting, for the first time, ASEAN was given an explicitly political character. A secretariat for the organization has now been opened in Jakarta, in keeping with the keystone role Indonesia, as the most populous of the member nations, expects to play. To date, there has not been any formal contact between ASEAN and the United States although there has been a limited formal dialogue between the organization and the European Economic Community as well as with Japan. The question of direct contact with the United States is sensitive because of Indochinese suspicion that ASEAN is a tool of American interests.

No regional issue concerns ASEAN nations so much as the intentions of Vietnam, now the strongest military power by far in the region. Last July Phan Hien, Deputy Foreign Minister of Vietnam, visited throughout the region in an apparent effort to establish closer bilateral relations with the non-Communist nations in the area. However, in September, at the Colombo Non-Aligned Conference, Laos, supported by Vietnam, succeeded in defeating a Malaysian effort to win the Conference's endorsement of a Southeast Asian zone of peace, freedom and neutrality. During the conference debate Vietnam's Foreign Minister Nguyen Duy Trinh sought to assure the ASEAN

representatives that its support for Laos' position should not be interpreted as a change in its policy to seek normalization of relations
with nations in the area. Nevertheless, Laos' action, founded on lingering suspicion that ASEAN is a covert device for continued American
intervention, rearoused fears over Vietnam and its Indochinese allies'
intentions, concerns that had been somewhat quieted by Phan Hien's
earlier visits. But the surface reaction was mild and, with the exception
of Thailand where the October military coup changed the picture, the
trend toward easing tensions between ASEAN nations and Vietnam
continues. Some observers see ASEAN-Indochina relations developing
along lines of the economic cooperation between Western and Eastern
Europe, envisioning economic ties between the two groupings to that
extent.

Thus far China has taken a detached view of ASEAN but no doubt
would view with concern any tendency to convert the organization
into a military alliance. Until the recent coup in Bangkok, China's
relations with Thailand were warming rapidly. Since then a distinct
chill has set in. Relations between China and the Philippines are
good and with Malaysia they are correct but cool. Indonesia, which
suspended diplomatic relations with China following Sukarno's ouster
from power, is still watching and waiting to restore contact, fearing
the possible impact an official Chinese presence could have on its
Chinese community. Singapore waits a move from Indonesia. Taiwan
has no embassies in the ASEAN countries but any step by China to
take Taiwan by force would be seen as an upsetting development
throughout the area.

Although ASEAN has not yet settled any of the inter-regional disputes that vex the region, such as the dormant Philippine claim to
Sabah and the Thai Muslim separatist movement, the growing value
all members attach to ASEAN harmony and goodwill helps dampen
down these old disputes and may have kept new ones from arising.

Progress by ASEAN on economic cooperation has been slow,
primarily because the member states are at different stages of development. The more developed members, Singapore and the Philippines,
favor a regional free trade policy in which they see themselves as the
bankers and manufacturers for the rest of the area. The less developed
members, led by Indonesia, wish to protect their own developing industries and are wary of penetration by trans-national enterprises,
which tend to be dominated by the overseas Chinese.

Specific ASEAN industrial projects are being developed. Basic
agreement has been reached on building plants to serve area-wide
needs for fertilizer, soda ash, and diesel engines. However, many details remain to be worked out on these projects, including the fundamental question of tariff preferences for the products. An initial step
toward cooperation on regional banking matters was recently taken
when the first ASEAN Bankers Conference agreed to establish an
ASEAN Bankers Council whose objective would be "to formulate
policy for coordination and cooperation among ASEAN bankers for
the development of the ASEAN region." The first concrete act was
agreement to set up a regional bank clearing arrangement. These steps,
small though they may be, are building blocks for cooperation on other
matters of common interest.

A strong economic development oriented ASEAN, tied to no major
power, could be an important factor in the future of Southeast Asia.

United States policy should be to encourage regional cooperation but to refrain from trying to force the pace or direction of the movement. As a result of past American policy in the region, principally the attempt to create non-neutral regimes which were strictly aligned in policy with the United States, nations now find it disadvantageous to be identified too closely with U.S. interests. What the United States needs in Southeast Asia over the long run are not weak nations tied to American purse strings but independent, neutral nations which cooperate to advance common, peaceful objectives. In the interest of regional stability and world peace, cooperation between the nations of ASEAN and Vietnam, Laos, and Cambodia is much to be desired. Perhaps eventually Burma can be brought into such an arrangement. However, strong animosities still exist within the region, centering on Thailand and Vietnam. Thailand's role in the Vietnam war makes it highly suspect to its Indochinese neighbors and the long history of troubles between it and Burma places it in a key position for encouraging or discouraging the expansion of regional cooperation.

The October coup in Thailand was a serious blow to budding efforts to heal the war wounds with the nations of Indochina. In the name of stability, a situation has been created that may well lead to increased instability. The departure of American forces from Thai bases three months before the coup was a sound move for both Thailand and for long-range American policy in the region. There is no justification in terms of our national interest, intelligence gathering or otherwise, which could possibly warrant the return of an American military presence to Thailand. Any resumption of U.S. operations in Thailand would inevitably be used to tie the United States to the policies of the current military regime. The discontent of poverty cannot be cured by guns and the efforts to do so promise only further rebellion in the poor, neglected rural areas.

The United States is still tied to Thailand by the moribund SEATO Treaty. One of the first priorities of the new Administration should be to review this vestige of our misguided post-World War II policy in Southeast Asia before it gets the nation into further difficulty.

II. PHILIPPINES

Following my 1975 visit to the Philippines I reported to the Committee that:

The Philippine Republic is experiencing a period of growing national assertion and economic progress. At the same time, its ties with the United States which go back three-quarters of a century are in transition. What is involved in this transition of principal concern to the United States are the vestiges of the previous dependency relationship which, in my judgment, no longer accord with the enduring interests of either nation. There is a need for a reshaping of attitudes and arrangements which will reflect the changes that have taken place within the Philippines and in the Pacific and the world. The future of the Philippines is bright and so, too, can be the outlook for continued cooperation and beneficial interchange with the United States if the adjustments which are now required are made in good time and are managed with sensitivity and understanding—on both sides.

The Philippines is now charting a course of independence and neutrality which seeks to maintain good relations with all of the major powers and identify the Philippines with the Third World. Self-reliance and national pride are stressed, exemplified in the nation's rejection of external assistance following the earthquake and tidal wave which struck the Philippines last August.

The year 1976 marked the fourth of martial law rule by President Ferdinand E. Marcos. There seems to be no widespread sorrow in the Philippines over the loss of the prior system. Martial law appears to be tolerated by most. A measure of law and order has been brought about and there has been the beginning of a concentrated attack on deep-rooted social problems. A great handicap of the past, the lack of a sense of national identity, is being tackled and national pride stimulated in various ways. Technocrats in the government are being given greater authority and recognition and more expertise is being sought to bring to bear on social problems.

The Muslim insurgency in the southern islands is less an active problem than in the past but it continues, as does the Communist insurgency in Central Luzon. The insurgencies are an economic, financial, and political drain on the government. The bulk of the Philippine army is tied down on Mindanao and nearby islands. The level of military activity has been reduced but, to date, there has been no real political dialogue between the government and the Muslim insurgents or political and economic change sufficient to satisfy the Muslims. It was recently agreed, however, that talks with the insurgents would commence through the auspices of Libya which has been a factor in financing the Muslim revolt. This is a hopeful sign and may possibly result in progress toward a solution to the dispute.

As to the general economic situation, the Philippines had a $1.2 billion trade deficit in 1975, a situation that is expected to continue for the next several years. Increased petroleum prices have taken a heavy toll on the Philippines' balance-of-payments situation with the cost of petroleum imports rising from $245 million in 1974 and to an estimated $1 billion this year.

The economic growth rate for 1976 will be approximately 6 percent while inflation is running at about 5.4 percent, considerably better than in 1975. The World Bank has estimated that in the 1980's the Philippines will need $9 billion in external financing above retained earnings but the country's debt-service burden is already high at 16 percent of exports and is expected to increase to 18 percent by 1980.

One of the most difficult problems facing the Philippines is the brain drain. The Republic has a very literate population and a well-trained managerial class but there is an outflow of trained Filipinos. It is estimated, for example, that there are some 25,000 Filipino doctors and 45,000 Filipino nurses in the United States. A developing country cannot afford such a loss and must find ways to stem this outflow of talent.

A rapidly growing population is one of the many problems facing the Philippines. From a population of 20 million in 1946 the number of Filipinos has escalated to 43 million today and the total is expected to reach 85 million or more by the turn of the century. Forty-three percent of the population is now under 15. Pressures are already such that some 700,000 to 800,000 jobs are needed each year for new job seekers and that requirement will grow to about one million by 1980. There is in these projections a great potential for discontent among young people over the next 10 to 15 years.

Food constituted some 10 percent of total imports. This year, however, the Philippines became self-sufficient in rice, thanks primarily to new strains of miracle rice, an improved farm credit system and other agricultural reforms. It is also self-sufficient in white corn. There is still a substantial shortage of feed grains. Large imports of wheat and other food products, amounted to some $242 million in 1974. The simple fact is that the Philippines must grow more food for more people on less land in the years ahead. In 1900 there were four hectares of land per person; now there are less than .8 per person.

President Marcos was an early advocate of family planning and his government recognizes that rapid population growth is the major impediment to economic and social progress. Public awareness of the population problem is great but, thus far, the government's emphasis on family planning has been in the cities although 70 percent of the people live in the rural areas. In five years the number of family planning clinics has gone from zero to 2,400.

As for economic relations between the United States and the Philippines, the Laurel-Langley agreement which set the framework for relations between the two countries in the postwar period expired two years ago and no successor agreement has been negotiated. In 1975 the Philippine exports to the United States were $655 million, smaller than the previous year because of lower commodity prices and smaller sugar imports. United States exports to the Philippines increased to $754 million bringing about a favorable balance for the United States for the first time in many years. The United States is the Philippines second largest trading partner after Japan. Japan has also replaced the United States as the leading investor although U.S. investments in the period from 1970 to 1975 were double that of Japan. The total market value of U.S. investments is some $2 billion, although they are only $1 billion at book value. Little American capital is now going into the Philippines except for investments in banks.

There have been informal talks between the two countries about a successor agreement to the Laurel-Langley agreement. The Philippines is interested in trade concessions while the United States' primary interest is in investment guaranties. The talks have now been suspended but are expected to resume in 1977.

Bilateral relations between the United States and the Philippines are presently focused on the base negotiations which began in Washington last April and moved back to the Philippines in June. The continued presence of the bases puts the Philippines in something of a difficult posture vis-a-vis ASEAN goals of independence and neutrality and the Philippines' policy of seeking a full-identification with the Third World. However, Filipinos recognize that the bases serve important mutual interests. The Chinese, concerned over Soviet influence in the Pacific, appear content to see the bases remain. I was told by one Chinese official in Peking:

We believe it is always not a good thing to have forces stationed on foreign soil. It seems your situation is also a result of the fact that you have interests to protect. As to how you go about that, it is a matter for you to decide.

Clark Air Base is the largest overseas military base of any country. The Subic Naval Base, a major station for servicing the Seventh Fleet, is the most important U.S. naval base west of Hawaii. U.S. military strategists consider the bases indispensible to a continued U.S. military presence in the Western Pacific. Some 16,000 U.S. servicemen are stationed on the bases, and they are joined by an additional 7,000-20,000 more at any one time from fleet units calling at Subic Bay.

Substantial sums are added to the Philippines' economy by the bases, $142 million last year, not including the multiplier effect of the spending. The acreage occupied by the bases is so vast that some 46,000 acres at Clark have been surplus to U.S. military needs for years. It is said that squatters on land at Clark raise sugar cane valued at some $10 million annually. Work that can be done at Subic costs $25 per man-day compared with $100 per man day for U.S. facilities in Japan and $200 per man-day in United States shipyards.

Both the United States and the Philippines recognize that the 1946 Base Agreement is obsolete. This agreement gives the United States the freest use of any foreign base in the world and, in effect amounts to a grant of extraterritorial rights. It is this question which is primarily at issue in the base negotiations. Other issues include financial payments, manner of usage and restraints on personnel. In brief, the problem is to attune the U.S. presence to the Filippino drive for full independence. One related problem concerns taxation of on-base commercial activities. The exchanges at the two bases do $65 million worth of business annually and goods passing through them often end up on the black market thus evading Filipino taxes, an operation that is extensive and well organized. It is said that an item which sells for one dollar in a base exchange will bring $2.50 on the black market.

The base negotiations are likely to remain in limbo until the new Administration assumes office in January. I am confident that satisfactory arrangements can be worked out thereafter. There are important mutual interests to be served by retaining the bases and on this common ground an agreement can be reached.

A matter of special note involves the Spratley Islands which lie to the West. With oil exploration a matter of growing regional friction, the islands are a potential source of difficulty in view of the existence of the U.S.-Philippines Mutual Securtiy Treaty. The Philippines Republic lays claim to the Spratleys as does the People's Republic of China, the Republic of China and Vietnam. There are troops from the Philippines, the Republic of China and Vietnam on one or more islands. A clarification or reconciliation of these claims without delay would seem to be in the interest of all concerned.

III. INDONESIA

Winds of change blow moderately in Indonesia, a land of 135 million people scattered among more than 3,000 islands extending East to West over a distance of 3,200 miles. Indonesia is the largest nation in Southeast Asia and the fifth most populous in the world. It is strategically located between Australia and the Asian mainland astride the sea lanes that link the Pacific and Indian Oceans. Continued unhindered transit of shipping through these waters is important to U.S. interests and is vital to Japan, for whom these waters are a lifeline to Europe and the Middle East.

Indonesia is a founder of the non-aligned movement. It is destined to play a leading role in Southeast Asia and throughout the developing world. Since Sukarno's fall from power a decade ago Indonesia has pursued a pragmatic approach to foreign policy. The stress has been on economic and social development as the best insurance of regional peace and security and the curbing of Communist influence. While

Indonesia frequently disagrees with U.S. policies, it has favored a cooperative approach toward the United States and other developed countries, opposing the confrontation tactics of many of the developing nations.

Led by men whose fear of Communism remains strong, Indonesia is taking a cautious approach toward relations with China and Vietnam. Although there are differences of viewpoint, the government of President Suharto has no present plans to resume diplomatic relations with the People's Republic of China which were suspended following Sukarno's fall and President Suharto's rise to power. There are deep-seated fears over the impact that a Chinese diplomatic presence could have on the three million local Chinese, especially in view of the fact that nearly one-third technically hold citizenship in the People's Republic of China. Indonesia is not concerned about direct action by China, but it is apprehensive over Hanoi's intentions, and is especially worried about the smuggling of arms into the country.

As the most populous and powerful member of ASEAN, Indonesia sees the organization as a device to further regional economic progress. It is well aware that any attempt to bind ASEAN to military purposes would run against the tide in Southeast Asia. Indonesia contends that it is opposed in principle to any foreign bases in the region, but defers to the Philippines for handling the question of U.S. bases.

Indonesia has absorbed what was once Portuguese Timor. Following the outbreak of fighting among political factions in Timor in August 1975, the Portuguese lost effective control. A dominant position was assumed by the anti-Indonesia Fretelin group. Indonesia became concerned that an independent East Timor would constitute a threat to Indonesia's security by providing an opening for Communist influence and subversion. Indonesia began to provide assistance to local groups opposing Fretelin. Indonesian "volunteers" landed in Timor and rapidly pushed the Freteline forces out of the main population centers. A provisional government was established which petitioned Jakarta for incorporation of East Timor into Indonesia. Follwing Parliamentary apprval, East Timor formally became the 27th Province of Indonesia on July 17, 1976.

There are currently infrequent reports of small-scale guerrilla activity by Fretelin units in isolated areas of East Timor, but Indonesian forces are reported to be gradually bringing this under control. U.S.-supplied military equipment was used by Indonesian forces in the operation, without U.S. permission. That points up again a continuing problem in the enforcement of U.S. security assistance laws, a problem which deserves early attention by Congress and the new Administration.

The present party system in Indonesia reflects an effort to remove the political focus from Indonesia's deep ethnic and religious cleavages and to establish program-oriented politics. Former parties which accentuated these cleavages have been absorbed in two new organizations, the Development Union Party (PPP), composed of various Moslem groupings, and the Indonesian Democratic Party (PDI), composed of two Christian and three secular groupings. Concurrently the government has actively supported a new federation of functional (youth, Labor, farmer, women) groups called Golkar. This organization won 62.8 percent of the votes and 65 percent of the elected seats in the 1971 election and is generally regarded as the civilian successor to the armed forces as the principal political base for the government.

The National Parliament is composed of 360 elected and 100 appointed members. Although Parliament seldom rejects government proposals it does have a voice in formulating them through prior committee consultations. The next parliamentary elections are scheduled for May 2, 1977. The President will be elected for a five-year term in the succeeding year by the People's Consultative Assembly, which consists of Parliament and an equal number of appointed members. The People's Consultative Assembly will also at that time adopt broad guidelines for governmental policy during the following five years.

Strongest opposition to the Suharto Government appears centered among adherents of former Moslem parties who claim that the most popular Moslem leaders have not been permitted to participate in leadership of the Development Union Party and that neither their electoral strength nor their views are properly reflected in the government. Criticism of the Suharto Government by these and other dissatisfied elements has centered on corruption. There seems to be, however, no basic disagreement with the Government's basic development policy goals.

Indonesia, one of the world's poorest nations in terms of per capita income, is richly endowed with a diversity of natural resources. It has important desposits of oil, natural gas, nickel, copper and tin and is a major producer of rubber, lumber and other agricultural products. Although the United States is not as heavily dependent as most industrial nations on these resources, circumstances could make them more important in the future. The United States' principal ally in Asia, Japan, relies heavily on Indonesian energy and raw materials. American firms have invested approximately $2.5 billion in Indonesia, primarily in oil and mining, and Indonesia welcomes further outside investment. There are, however, severe restraints on the development of Indonesia's minerals and, to a lesser extent, timber resources. These are traditionally capital-intensive industries. For example, the Shell Group recently entered into a production-sharing agreement with the state-owned coal mining company to exploit extensive coal deposits in Sumatra for which the development costs are expected to exceed $1.2 billion. Much of Indonesia's abundant mineral resources are located in the most inaccessible, primative parts of Indonesia. Everywhere development of Indonesia's resources is characterized by large capital expenditures. Even petroleum exploration and development costs, while not reaching North Sea levels, are far in excess of other OPEC member. While Indonesia has the potential resources which eventually could make it very strong economically, it is still some distance from self-sustaining growth.

Oil dominates the Indonesian economy; and following the doubling of world oil prices in late 1973 and 1974, there was much optimism about Indonesia's prospects. This optimism was dealt a severe blow by problems encountered in 1975. In that year there was decline in demand for Indonesia's exports; a severe cash crisis in the state-owned oil company, Pertamina; a drop in foreign investment; and continued high levels of inflation.

Indonesia's oil revenues add only marginally to one of the world's lowest per capita annual income rates and Indonesia, which accounts for only about five percent of OPEC's oil production, has about half of OPEC's population. Ninety percent of Indonesia's oil is produced by U.S. companies.

Pertamina is responsible under Indonesian law for managing all petroleum activities in the country, including exploration, production, refining and marketing. It owns and operates all of Indonesia's refineries, domestic distribution facilities, and a fleet of tankers and other vessels; it is also involved in a variety of non-petroleum activities. Under the leadership of its former president, Lt. General Ibnu Sutowo, Pertamina became the leading edge of the government's development schemes. Pertamina's financial crisis surfaced publicly in early 1975, when it began having difficulties rolling over some of its short-term obligations. Rather than risk default and the attendant damage to Indonesia's credit standing, the government stepped in and assumed responsibility for Pertamina's debts, which totaled more than $6 billion. Observers credit the government with effective handling of the Pertamina crisis but in the process Indonesia has greatly increased its debt burden. Debt service will approach the IMF "warning level" of 20 percent of total value of exports in the 1979–80 period. As a fallout of the Pertamina crisis, President Suharto announced in his budget message of January 7, 1976, that government revenues would be increased by 7.6 percent, and that this increase would mainly be "acquired through reduction of profits gained by oil companies on each barrel they produce." There then ensued a complex series of negotiations with foreign oil companies, characterized in many instances by a confrontational atmosphere. Under the new oil contract terms, Indonesia achieved an 85–15 profit (formerly 65–35) which should increase its revenues by $350 million, or expressed another way, Indonesia's take increased an average of $1.88 per barrel of oil, from $6.19 per barrel to $8.07.

In a separate, but related development, Indonesia recently has spoken in a number of international meetings on economic problems as seen by the Third World. Although its leaders continue to seek large infusions of foreign capital, they have become more responsive to domestic and foreign criticism that foreign investment amounts to "selling out the country." Because of the importance of primary products to Indonesia's economy, Indonesia is particularly concerned about better terms of trade, higher value being added in producer countries, producer control of transport and marketing, and other portions of the platform of the new world economic order. Nonetheless, while identifying strongly with the Third World, Indonesia has generally sought to play a moderating role in that group.

Indonesia has had one of the highest rates of inflation in the world over the last five years. Although the rate has declined somewhat over the past 12 months, it is currently running at approximately 20 percent per annum, significantly higher than neighboring countries and trade competitors. As a consequence, the exchange rate of the rupiah, which was set at 415 to the dollar in 1971, is under considerable pressure. Indonesia's net foreign reserves declined seriously during 1975, reaching a low point of $442 million in the third quarter of 1975. Reserves have since staged a recovery, and as of mid-August 1976, were reported at $1.1 billion.

Indonesia has over 135 million people living at the subsistence level and a very poorly developed economic and social infrastructure. Its trade balance has been persistently in deficit, even after oil prices rose sharply in 1974. In the first Indonesian fiscal year after the oil price rise there was a trade deficit of $138 million which rose to nearly $1 billion in the last fiscal year. The International Monetary Fund projects a $1.8 billion deficit for the current fiscal year, which will be reduced somewhat by the increased take from oil profits.

Despite increased earnings from oil exports, Indonesia continues to depend on large amounts of external aid. Economic assistance to Indonesia is coordinated through the Inter-Governmental Group on Indonesia (IGGI), formed in 1967 with the purpose of helping the Suharto Government obtain external financing for Indonesia's development program. The IGGI is composed of fourteen countries, the World Bank, International Monetary Fund, and the Asian Development Bank. Through FY 1974 the U.S. and Japan each pledged under the umbrella of the IGGI to provide one-third of Indonesia's bilateral aid requests. In FY 1975 the U.S. abandoned the one-third formula with a significant reduction in its pledge. The World Bank has become the largest donor agency to Indonesia with a commitment target for FY 1977 of $550 million. Japan, providing about $140 million this year, is the largest bilateral donor.

There is no end in sight to Indonesia's need for external assistance, according to the development assistance community. The U.S. has provided some $2.2 billion in assistance to Indonesia since independence. It appears to me that the large volume of assistance, especially food aid, has served as a crutch which has helped Indonesia avoid facing up to its own internal problems, particularly those relating to food production. By providing subsidized food to make up the self-sufficiency gap, the United States and other aid donors have enabled Indonesia to avoid making hard choices in national priorities of development.

The contrast between Indonesia's vast numbers of poor and the few rich is typified in Jakarta where a short distance off broad boulevards lined by huge new office buildings and hotels, lie wretched slums. In the seven years since my last visit to Indonesia there does not appear to have been any progress toward narrowing the gap between the rich and the poor. If anything, the disparity has been made more glaring, at least in the capital, by a facade of modernity and progress.

There is no land shortage in Indonesia, only an overconcentration of population. Two-thirds of its population live on two islands, Java and Bali. Java, with 1,500 persons per square mile, is one of the most densely populated areas in the world. However, there is no program at present to encourage migration to the less developed islands and the population pressures on Java and Bali mount. Indonesia is still dependent on imports to meet its needs for rice. Rice imports will total about one million tons this year, with 350,000 tons to come from the United States financed under the PL 480 program or on long-term credits.

There is an effective population planning program. It is said that five years ago the annual population growth rate was three percent; has now been reduced to 2.3 percent and the goal is to reduce it to 1.8 percent by the end of 1979. There are strong social pressures to participate in the birth control program through local "Mother's Clubs."

With the advent of the Suharto Government in 1967, the United States resumed military assistance. The first post-Sukarno era U.S.

military assistance project consisted of a modest civic action program aimed at displaying U.S. support for the new regime, a program to assist the armed forces to rehabilitate roads, ports, and irrigation systems. Military grant aid in FY 1967 amounted to only $2.7 million. In 1970, following President Nixon's visit to Indonesia and support from it for the U.S. policy in Cambodia, U.S. military assistance multiplied and changed in character. A 1971 interagency study set as a planning guide $25 million in MAP grant aid for each of the next five years, and aid continued at approximately this level for several years until it was reduced following general cutbacks in military aid by Congress.

Today, the U.S. Diplomatic Mission to Indonesia is staffed by a total of 231 Americans. The military mission of 70 has increased more than five-fold since my last visit in 1969. The U.S. mission, in my judgment, is overstaffed and should be trimmed back substantially.

In summary, American relations with Indonesia are good but the relationship is not as close as in the initial post-Sukarno years and it is likely to become more distant in the days ahead.

IV. MALAYSIA

Although Malaysia has a strong Western orientation, the government's official policy has been to cultivate the Third World and to take an active part in nonaligned affairs. Since 1971, it has also advocated creation of a zone of peace, freedom and neutrality in Southeast Asia and supported the proposal for an Indian Ocean peace zone. Non-alignment and support for zones of peace and neutrality are intended to insulate Malaysia, if possible, from the effects of great power rivalry in the region and in the world at large. They are also intended to give the government some leverage on international economic developments.

In 1960 the Malayan "emergency" was declared to be officially at an end, although long before this Malaysian Communist Party (MCP) Secretary Chin Peng had withdrawn the remnants of his terrorist forces across the border into Thailand. The MCP set out in 1968/69 to re-establish itself in Malaysia by sending small groups of armed terrorists back across the border to attack government security forces and to activate old underground networks in the cities and new Chinese settlements. The MCP has had some success in its campaign, but increased government counter-insurgency efforts and a split in the MCP itself have slowed this activity markedly. It is estimated that there are some 3,000 active and armed terrorists in all. At present, the terrorists are a nagging and expensive annoyance but they do not pose a threat to the government or to the daily life of the country at large.

The U.S. has no major programs in Malaysia. There has never been an aid program, a military assistance agreement or bases. The Peace Corps with approximately 60 volunteers is the largest U.S. program. It is designed to supply experts to fill gaps in government programs in education, health and agriculture pending the training of Malaysians. In addition to the Peace Corps, the United States has a small military training program through which 40 to 60 Malaysian service personnel are sent to the U.S. each year for training. There also is a military credit program which amounted to $17 million in fiscal year 1976 and will total approximately $5 million in fiscal year 1977, financing items such as F–5E and F–5B aircraft, C–130 transports, helicopters and armored cars.

Relations between Washington and Kuala Lumpur are cordial but not intimate. Prime Minister Datuk Hussein Onn has publicly expressed his desire to see a continued U.S. economic and diplomatic presence in Southeast Asia but his government is also conscious of the need to preserve its distance from all of the major powers. It maintains correct relations with both the Soviet Union and the People's Republic of China and has offered technical assistance to Vietnam. It sent an ambassador to Hanoi in October. Although Malaysia is concerned about Vietnam, it sees no alternative to bringing it into association with the other nations of Southeast Asia.

The United States is one of Malaysia's most important customers, taking, for example, 40 percent of its most significant export, natural rubber. Bilateral trade in 1975 involved exports to this country of rubber, tin, palm oil and timber products amounting to $536 million. Malaysia imported $394 million worth of U.S. machinery and transportation equipment, manufactured goods, chemicals and other products during that same year. U.S. investment in Malaysia rose to an estimated $450 million in 1975. The main component is petroleum exploration and exploitation but the investments also involve extensive participation in the electronics industry.

All signs point to continued economic expansion. Financial reserves are ample, the country is a preferred borrower. The security problem is currently manageable. If peace and stability in the region continue, Malaysia prospects are encouraging for the foreseeable future.

V. SINGAPORE

Singapore, a city state of some 3 million, has utilized its geographical location, its excellent harbor, and a skilled populace to reach a level of development unparalleled in Southeast Asia. Singapore's $2,500 per capita GNP is exceeded in Asia only by Japan. Its well-being is dependent on the state of the world economy and on the cooperation of its neighbors, Indonesia and Malaysia, which provide the goods and markets for the Singapore entrepot and the raw materials for Singapore's factories.

Seventy-six percent of Singapore's population are descendents of the Chinese migrants who for centuries have moved to Southeast Asia in search of greater opportunity. Both Malaysia and Indonesia also have Chinese minorities (36 percent in Malaysia, about three percent in Indonesia) which dominate their commerce and are visibly wealthier than the ethnic majorities. In both countries there is a heritage of mistrust and tension between the Malay/Indonesian and the ethnic Chinese communities, reflected in varying degrees in the attitudes of their governments toward Singapore.

Although Premier Lee Kuan Yew, who has been in power for seventeen years, visited Peking last May, Singapore has not yet established formal diplomatic relations with China, stating that it will not do so until after Indonesia has acted. Singapore is an active member of ASEAN and has pressed for the elimination of trade barriers and greater economic cooperation, to the discomfort, in particular, of less economically developed Indonesia. Internationally, Singapore is ostensibly non-aligned. Its commitment to free enterprise and its reliance on the world market, however, have given its policies a generally pro-Western bias. In its security relationships, for example, Singapore has until recently looked primarily to the Five-Power Defense Arrangement (FPDA) that links it—along with Malaysia—to Britain, Australia and New Zealand. Last March, Britain completed withdrawal from its naval base in Singapore. However, a small New Zealand Army unit is still based there.

Singapore's vulnerability, especially to outside economic pressures, requires the government to exercise special care in not antagonizing other countries unnecessarily. For example, the dependence of the huge Singapore oil refining complex, third largest in the world, on Middle East crude is a prime element in shaping Singapore's cautiously neutral position toward Arab-Israeli issues. Prime Minister Lee has been outspoken about the importance of maintaining a great power balance in the region. He believes that the Soviets will not voluntarily limit their presence in the area and that, therefore, there should be no pressure on the United States to leave the region. Indeed, Lee has implied that it is necessary to encourage the United States to maintain a suitable presence both in Southeast Asia, as well as in the Indian Ocean.

The attitude of Lee and his government toward the presence of the major powers in Southeast Asia stems in part from Singapore's position as an ethnic Chinese city-state. Aware of the potential pull of the Chinese homeland, Lee has been reluctant to follow the Malaysians, Thais and Filipinos in establishing relations with Peking. On the other hand, because Singapore is situated in an area dominated ethnically by Malays, Lee prefers the region to be open to the peaceful competition of the great powers provided no single power is dominant.

Since the communist victory in Indochina, Lee has looked to the United States for support in the security field. He is especially concerned over the implications of the insurgency in Malaysia. Modern equipment has been procured in the United States on commercial terms. Singapore recently contracted to purchase a squadron of F-5E's with air-to-air missiles. Singapore's decision to acquire a substantial portion of its military equipment and service requirements from the United States is consonant with the overall cordial bilateral relationship. Singapore is not only a major trading and investment partner of the United States, it also grants this Nation access to its naval and air facilities. Soviet ships also bunker and replenish at Singapore's docks. Chinese ships also stop there.

Because of the "openness" of the economy, Singapore is extremely vulnerable to foreign trade fluctuations. The manufacturing and foreign trade sectors have been seriously impacted by the world recession and the shrinkage in international trade. But barring unforeseen circumstances, there should be a six to eight percent increase in economic growth in 1976. Inflation has not been a problem recently, amounting only to three percent in 1975.

Singapore maintains one of the most attractive investment climates in East Asia. There are no significant limitations on foreign equity participation or in the employment of expatriate management staffs. Financial inducements, usually in the form of tax forgiveness, are available to those companies engaged in lines of production involving high technology and intensive capital investment. Responding to these enticements and to the advantages offered by Singapore's location and its efficient administration, American private investment stands at nearly $1 billion. It constitutes the island's single largest source of private foreign investment. It is estimated that one-fourth to one-third of the Americans in Singapore are there in connection with oil drilling operations in the area but, because of a falloff in activity, their population may be reduced by one-half in coming years. Twenty drilling rigs are now in mothballs.

Singapore is eligible for preferences under U.S. tariff laws and in response to a request of the Singapore government, the product eligibility rules were broadened recently to take Singapore's entrepot economy into account.

VI. PAPUA NEW GUINEA

Newly independent Papua New Guinea is an important bridge between Southeast Asia and the Southwest Pacific, with 85 percent of its land area made up of the eastern half of the massive island of New Guinea. Irian Jaya, the western half, is a province of Indonesia.

American missionaries have been in New Guinea for decades and more than 2,500 are there today. Over a million American servicemen went through Papua New Guinea during the Second World War and they are remembered with fondness. General Douglas MacArthur is recalled with special respect.

While the United States does not have any vital interests in Papua New Guinea, the nation plays a role in U.S. objectives for the Pacific. U.S. strategic interests in the area are supported by the maintenance of harmonious and cooperative relationships between Papua New Guinea and Australia and Indonesia; the denial of bases and other local facilities to potential enemies; and the continuation of the country's political unity and stability.

The U.S. Mission is small, highly regarded and effective. Papua New Guinea's leadership is well disposed toward the United States, and has pursued moderate internal and foreign policies. There is no U.S. aid program, not even a Peace Corps presence and in my judgment it should remain this way.

Papua New Guinea became a sovereign nation on September 16, 1975. Its leaders have since demonstrated a capacity to lead the country effectively even when confronted with a number of difficult problems, including a secessionist movement on the copper-rich island of Bougainville. Several important economic developments have occurred during the past year. For Papua New Guinea, the most crucial was an aid commitment by the Government of Australia for $1.2 billion over the next five years. The Government of Papua New Guinea has encouraged direct foreign investments under increasingly hospitable terms. Moreover, during the period of economic stagnation and decline in revenues from basic commodities, not once did the Government attempt to align itself with the more extreme positions of the Third World to curtail supplies or attempt to manipulate the market by artificially created higher prices.

Papua New Guinea is one of the world's least tapped sources of natural resources. Copper, gold, silver and zinc are some of the minerals known to exist in commercially profitable quantities. Gas has been found, and oil is thought to be there. A wide variety of tropical produce can be grown. Access to tuna fishing grounds and timber resources are eagerly sought after by foreign companies. The ratio of resources to its population is very favorable. With fewer than three million people and a population density of seven persons per square mile, Papua New Guinea is much more favorably endowed than most developing countries. Economic aid from Australia has provided the basis for the beginnings of the infrastructure without significant international indebtedness.

The present government has had almost five years' experience in running the country; the country's political institutions are operative; the army has stayed out of politics and is loyal to the government; the country is at peace with its neighbors; its international problems are minor; there is a strong egalitarian tradition among the people; and there are no ideological hangups.

On the other hand, Papua New Guinea suffers from difficult divisions of geography and language and from wide variations in degree of development. The rapid pace of modernization is leaving large sections far behind, with sophisticated political and economic systems imposed on a primitive tribal society. Only 15 percent of the people are literate. The leadership of the country is painfully small in number, and the supply of trained manpower is quite inadequate. The people have high expectations. Tremendous opportunities which are available to trained young people are leading them to focus more on their own careers than on the country's future. An elite has been created which could easily become divided from the people.

The government is beginning to display greater receptivity to foreign private investment. Several large projects are now pending and, if approved, they will eventually provide tax revenue, export earnings, and jobs. The lead time for most of them is six to ten years, but they will require construction workers to build roads, bridges and houses before becoming operational. The projects now under construction include a U.S. Steel sponsored gold mine ($200 million), three copper mines which will be developed by international consortia, and a fish canning project. In addition, natural gas exploration is being conducted by a Japanese consortium and oil drilling is taking place in three localities under the aegis of a U.S./Australian/British consortium. Further down the road is an enormous hydro-electric project which will require billions of dollars to develop but which is expected to create large amounts of relatively cheap electricity.

Papua New Guinea is an inward-looking country absorbed in its own affairs. It is at peace with its neighbors and has no pressing problems of foreign policy. Its basic policy has been described as one of having "no friends and no enemies." The government does not want to be involved in great power struggles and does not want aid from the United States, the Soviets or the Chinese. "We are neutral to everybody;" a national leader said to me, "if you come as friends, we are not interested in ideology." The nations most relevant to Papua New Guinea's future are Australia, Indonesia and Japan. Australia is important because of the long and close association, a very large aid program and the significant role of Australian business in the economy. Indonesia is important because it shares the boundary which divides Papua New Guinea from the Melanesians of Irian Jaya. Japan is of growing importance as a main competitor with Australia in the

nation's economic relations. Papua New Guinea also has close ties
with the other small Pacific island countries. Ethnic and emotional
considerations enter into these ties but in economic terms, it is becoming increasingly evident that the Philippines and Indonesia will be of
far greater significance than the coral atolls of the Pacific.

Papua New Guinea is pursuing a foreign policy of fostering a correct friendship with larger countries and avoiding the making of
enemies. It is likely to stay somewhat apart from the Afro-Asian bloc
countries, and to abstain from involvement in issues not directly affecting the South Pacific. It has diplomatic relations with both the
Soviet Union and China, but there is concern over the possibility of a
Soviet presence in Tonga and the Chinese presence in Western Samoa.

With its great and developed natural resources and its proximity to
resource-poor Japan, it is also concerned with that nation's economic
dominance in the region. There is interest in having the United States
and other nations increase their economic involvement as a balancing
factor, "Investment possibilities are here," a leader said to me: "Mention anything, we have it here." Papua New Guinea is, in truth, a
storehouse of vast potential in a world of dwindling resources as well
as a bridge between Southeast Asia and Southwest Pacific. It wants
outside capital for resource development, but only on its terms.

While it is a new nation with many problems, Papua New Guinea
is taking the long view in its relations with the world. "We are
friends," Sir Maori Kiki, the Acting Prime Minister said to me. I
hope that the relationship between our countries will remain cordial.
There are no outstanding contentious issues between us and there exists
a wide basis of understanding.

VII. Concluding Comments

Since this report completes the general survey of U.S. policy in
Asia and the Pacific which I began last July, I will conclude with a
number of comments about certain specific matters which relate to
that policy.

American policy in Asia is now grounded on the fact that the
United States is not an Asian power but a Pacific power. The difference is more than semantic. It is the difference between a sensible acceptance of the realities of Asia and dangerous illusions of military
omnipotence. What takes place in the vast region of Asia, of course, is
of concern to Americans. But concern and control are quite different
matters. Simply stated, America's principal long-range interests in the
Pacific are to discourage domination of the region by any single power,
to maintain friendly relations with China, Japan and other nations
and to lessen tensions which could trigger either a local or a great
power conflict in the area.

In my estimation the United States position in Asia and the Pacific
is more favorable than it has been since the end of World War II:

There is no war.

We enjoy good relations with all nations except North Korea
and the countries of Indochina, which the Executive Branch has
chosen to ignore.

After the tragedy of Indochina, both we and the nations of the
region have a better understanding of what it takes to live in
peace in a diverse world.

There are no American troops in Southeast Asia or anywhere else on the Asian mainland except in South Korea where 40,000 remain.

The economic burden of U.S. political involvement in the area has lessened.

The foremost problem for American policy regarding Asia is to complete the normalization of relations with the People's Republic of China.

The partnership between the United States and Japan remains as a fundamental pillar of American policy in Asia. It must be a partnership of equality; the post-war era of patron-client is over. Japan's continued trust in the validity of the United States security commitment is essential to the maintenance of stability throughout the region. This country ought not to provide the grounds for Japanese to doubt the U.S. security guarantee or to make a significant change in their domestic policy. A Japan embarked on major military expansion would unsettle all of Asia. U.S.-Japan relations are good but they could be better and it behooves us to avoid the further shocks of sudden policy shifts without notice.

Korea is a time bomb which must be defused. The United States' objective should be to try to bring about a settlement between the two Koreas and, in the interim, to ease tensions and lessen the possibility for a resumption of hostilities. U.S. policy should not be hostage to any particular government in Korea, or anywhere else for that matter. Our forces in this last U.S. bastion on the Asian Mainland should be reduced over a period of time, after consultation with Japan, and all nuclear weapons should be removed from the peninsula.

In Southeast Asia, the foremost task for U.S. policy remains to adjust to the realities in Indochina. The current policy of opposition to trade and diplomatic relations with Vietnam and Cambodia and to Vietnam's application for membership in the United Nations, as well as the failure to send an Ambassador to Laos has something in it of the ostrich complex. The fact is that just as China was not ours to lose in 1949, neither was Indochina a quarter of a century later. It is time that the United States act toward the governments of Indochina in a spirit which seeks to heal the wounds of war and therefore, enhances the prospect for a final accounting of the missing in action. Vietnam is a major force in Southeast Asia and it is in this nation's long-range interest to accommodate to that fact.

The remnants of a long-time U.S. military involvement, a smouldering insurgency in the Northeast, a genuine fear of North Vietnam's intentions, and the continued existence of the SEATO treaty commitment to Thailand, all add up to a sensitive and volatile situation for the United States in Thailand. There should be no resumption of the vast array of U.S. activities once carried out in Thailand, and the SEATO commitment should be terminated.

The era of U.S. military adventure on the Asian Mainland is over. We now have a more realistic view of what, as a practical matter, can and cannot be done on that continent. We know that it is not possible, or even desirable, to remake ancient cultures in our own image. There is a sober realization of the limits of America's resources and power. As was true of America in the past, the America of the future will be the beacon to the world, not because of military might or foreign aid but because of what it stands for in furthering aspirations for freedom and human decency.

There is an agenda of unfinished business in Asia and the Pacific, to be sure. But the problems are manageable. What is needed is the will to clear away the last relics of out-dated policies, to learn from the past, and to face up to the present and the future.

CHINA ENTERS THE POST-MAO ERA

LETTER OF TRANSMITTAL

NOVEMBER 18, 1976.

Hon. JOHN SPARKMAN,
Chairman, Committee on Foreign Relations,
U.S. Senate, Washington, D.C.

DEAR MR. CHAIRMAN: With the Committee's approval, and the support of President Ford and Secretary of State Kissinger, I visited the People's Republic of China from September 21, 1976, through October 12, 1976, as a guest of the Chinese People's Institute of Foreign Affairs. Transmitted herewith is a report of that trip. A confidential report was submitted to President Ford when I met with him on November 5th.

This visit was my sixth to China; it was the third since the new relationship was begun by President Nixon in 1972. A span of half-a-century between the first and the most recent provides a basis for perspective.

While in China in late September and early October, I had the opportunity to travel widely, covering some 9,000 miles by plane, train, car, and boat. Through the courtesy of my Chinese hosts, I was privileged to enter areas in China not visited since 1949 by Americans, such as certain localities in the Xinjiang (Sinkiang) Region, and other places not visited by any official American group as, for example, parts of Jiangsu (Kiangsu) and Guangdong (Kwangtung) Provinces. The Chinese people were warm and gracious in their hospitality, anxious to accommodate and to display local accomplishments.

China is a vast, underdeveloped, resource-rich land of industrious and talented people who comprise some one-fourth the population of the globe. Chinese influence on the rest of the world, already substantial, will increase greatly in the decades ahead. It is essential that U.S. policy be shaped to that reality. I know of no greater service that I could render to the American people in the time remaining in my third of a century of service in the Congress than to contribute to bringing about better understanding of the People's Republic of China and a normalization of relations with that nation.

I was accompanied on the trip by Senator John Glenn and his wife, Anna, both of whom contributed greatly to the mission. I wish to express my appreciation to the Department of State in Washington and in the field for assistance in arrangements throughout the course of the trip; the Department of the Air Force for transportation to and from China; Deputy Assistant Secretary of State Victor Dikeos for his efficient handling of logistics and other details during the trip; my assistant Mrs. Salpee Sahagian and Senator Glenn's secretary, Miss Kathy Prosser, for their able and willing help at all times; Dr. Thomas Lowe of the Navy Medical Corps for his services and his assistance in studying the Chinese system of health care; Mr. Francis R. Valeo, Secretary of the Senate, Mr. Charles R. Gellner, Senior Specialist in Foreign Affairs of the Congressional Research Service, Library of Congress, and Mr. Norvill Jones of the staff of the Committee on Foreign Relations, for their assistance.

To Madame Kang Tai-sha, Mr. Cheng Wan-chen, Mr. Fan Kuohsiang, Miss Tsung Chun, Mrs. Ku Yi-jen, and Mr. Yung, of the People's Institute of Foreign Affairs who accompanied my group during its travels in China, go my special thanks. Their great kindness, warmth, and good humor typify the people of China.

I also wish to express special appreciation to my wife, Maureen, for her usual helpful advice and good cheer throughout the trip.

Sincerely,

MIKE MANSFIELD.

LETTER FROM PRESIDENT FORD

THE WHITE HOUSE,
Washington, July 30, 1976.

Hon. MIKE MANSFIELD,
U.S. Senate,
Washington, D.C.

DEAR MIKE: One of the most helpful aspects of the resumption of friendly contact with the People's Republic of China has been the close collaboration between the Executive Branch and the Congress and the complete bipartisanship which has characterized the undertaking. As Majority Leader of the Senate, you and the Minority Leader have been principal participants in this process from the outset.

It has been almost two years since your last visit to the People's Republic of China, and I am pleased to hear that you have again been invited to visit that country. Your trip will provide a renewed demonstration of the bipartisan support in Congress for our policy of improving Sino-American relations. Of equal significance is the fact that you will be the first Member of Congress to make three trips to the People's Republic. This background makes you an unusually qualified observer, and I would find it most useful to receive another report from you containing your latest impression of developments in the People's Republic of China and your recommendations concerning those policies which you feel may be most appropriate at this time.

The Departments of the Executive Branch will, of course, be pleased to assist you in every appropriate way in connection with your visit.

Sincerely,

GERALD R. FORD.

CHINA ENTERS THE POST-MAO ERA

I. Introduction

I returned to China on September 21, 1976 for the sixth time while the nation was still in deep mourning over the death, on September 9, of Chairman Mao Tse-tung. For three weeks, I travelled approximately 9,000 miles within the country, by plane, train, car and boat.[1] While there I had an opportunity to talk to many Chinese leaders on the commune and factory and the national level. I had extensive discussions on foreign affairs and other matters with Vice Premier Li Hsien-nien, Vice Minister of Foreign Affairs Wang Hai-jung, T'ang Wen-sheng, Deputy Director of the American and Oceanian Affairs Department of the Ministry of Foreign Affairs, Dr. Chou Pei-yuan, Vice Chairman of the People's Institute of Foreign Affairs, and, at the provincial level, with Mr. Ismayil Aymat, Vice Chairman of the Xinjiang (Sinkiang)[2] Region's Revolutionary Committee and Mr. Feng Kuo-chu, Vice Chairman of the Shanghai Municipal Revolutionary Committee.

The Year of the Dragon has been a year of upheaval for China. Both its landscape and the political scene were shaken by earthquakes. The year 1976 witnessed the death of three giants of the Chinese Revolution, all comrades on the Long March, Premier Chou En-lai, Marshall Chu Teh, and the architect of the new China, Chairman Mao Tse-tung. It saw also the cashiering of Vice Premier Teng Hsiao-peng, the rise from obscurity of Hua Kuo-feng, Mao's successor as party chairman, and the denunciation of a number of leaders of the party. Once more political events in China have surprised the outside experts.

Although the official mourning period for Chairman Mao ended on September 18, widespread unofficial mourning continued until October 1, China's national day, and beyond in some areas. From Peking to the rural areas of remote Xinjiang (Sinkiang) Region, the manifestations of loss were everywhere. In city and countryside, hundreds of millions of black armbands were worn during the mourning period. Factories, stores, schools, commune gates—practically every public facility—bore posters expressing grief at his passing. Crepe paper symbols of mourning adorned trucks, tractors, animals and carts. Never have I seen such widespread public manifestations at the death of a political figure. The personal loss obviously felt by so many was illustrated by the reaction of a veteran interpreter accompanying our group whose voice broke on a number of occasions when translating comments concerning Mao's passing. Wherever our group went, from fac-

---

[1] See Appendix A for a chronology and map of the visit.
[2] Throughout this report the official Chinest spelling of place names is used, followed in parentheses, if necessary for clarity, by the spelling commonly used in the West.

tory, commune and national leaders, we heard the refrain: "We shall turn grief into strength."

Throughout my stay, I saw no manifestations of civic unrest or political disorder, although there appeared to be more military personnel on the streets of Beijing (Peking) than had been the case in 1974. While I was in China, it was made known that Premier Hua Kuo-feng had been selected to succeed Mao as Chairman of the Central Committee of the Chinese Communist Party and as Chairman of the Military Commission which controls the armed forces. During the days prior to my departure from the country, wall posters appeared calling for public support of the party's decision.

Both when I left Washington and as I emerged from China the news media were engaged in another round of speculation about political maneuverings within the Chinese leadership. In the report to the Senate following my 1974 visit to China, I said:

> The constant speculation over what will happen in China after Chairman Mao Tse-tung retires from the scene, in my opinion, is largely an exercise in irrelevance. It ignores the depth and the reality of the revolutionary changes which have taken place in China during the last quarter century. Mao is esteemed almost to the point of reverence because he has pointed the way and his leadership has restored China's self-confidence. Mao's precepts can be expected to guide China's destiny for a long time to come. "Serve the people" and "self-reliance" are more than slogans, they are the guideposts of Chinese society for the present and future.[3]

It is highly unlikely that, for the foreseeable future, it will make any significant difference who controls China insofar as United States-China relations are concerned. "If we are to carry on the great cause of Chairman Mao," one high Chinese official said to me, "it means our internal and foreign policy will not change." The Mao legacy is large and no Chinese political figure will be able to stray far from the broad outlines of his policies, at home or abroad. The decision to build a memorial hall in Peking in which Mao's body will be enshrined will aid in perpetuating that legacy.

What is important to the American people about China is not the makeup of its leadership or who is on the way up or down. The significance of China's political scene is that the system Chairman Mao created for China is working. It is bringing about rapid advances throughout the land. It has harnessed the talents of 800 to 950 million people as never before in China's history to achieve common goals. These are the realities which carry great meaning for American foreign policy and the future course of the world.

I returned to the new China for this third visit in an effort to gain a deeper understanding of the meaning of the changes taking place in China. As the first American official to meet with Chinese leaders following Chairman Mao's death, I was there at a significant time for the course of American policy toward China in the months and years ahead. I came away with a strengthened conviction that America can and should come to terms with the realities of China without delay.

---

³ "China: A Quarter Century After the Founding of the People's Republic," Report to the Senate Committee on Foreign Relations, January 1975, p. 1.

II. The State of U.S.-China Relations

"What is past is prologue" and a comprehension of the State of U.S.-China relations today requires an understanding of the past.

American images of China have fluctuated and shifted over the years. In a 1968 speech at the University of Montana, I said:

> There has been the image of the China of Marco Polo, Pearl Buck, Charlie Chan, and heroic resistance to the Japanese during World War II.
>
> On the other hand there has been the image of the China of cruelty, barbarism, violence, and faceless hordes. This is the China of drumhead trials, summary executions, Fu Manchu, and the Boxer Rebellion—the China that is summed up by the phrase "yellow peril."

These images of China have alternated until today. Since the beginning of United States contact with China two centuries ago, Americans feelings have been ambivalent. Generations of missionaries, traders, teachers, and travelers have created strong sentimental attachments to China which, on the one hand, provide a reservoir of goodwill and respect and, on the other, an attitude of superiority toward the Chinese. Paternalism has been the hallmark of American experience in China. Most Americans did not go to China to listen and learn but to preach, teach, and trade. They were the superiors, the Chinese the inferiors. Humanitarianism was mixed with a heavy blend of bigotry and greed.

Missionaries, not traders, did the most to shape American attitudes, toward China. It has been estimated that in 1925 there were 5,000 American missionaries in China. Their influence went far beyond their numbers, holding as they did key positions for the spread of western ideas and culture throughout the land. For decades until World War II, the pulpits of churches across America rang each Sunday with pleas for funds to feed, clothe, and save the souls of hundreds of millions of the "heathen" in China.

In the aftermath of World War II, admiration and affection turned to disappointment as the forces led by Chiang Kai-shek and Mao Tsetung resumed the civil war. American disappointment became hostility when the U.S.-supported Kuomintang armies were forced to retreat to the island of Taiwan in 1949. One consequence of this defeat was the poisoning of the American political system. A bitter personal debate began and lasted for years on the question: "Who lost China?" The ramifications were such that it resulted in a policy based on an official view that saw China as an aggressive, Soviet-dominated and directed giant posing a clear and present danger to its Asian neighbors. Secretary of State Dean Acheson, in releasing the Department of State's White Paper, said:

"The Communist leaders have foresworn their Chinese heritage and have publicly announced their subservience to a foreign power, Russia,...[4]

As late as 1960, in a television debate with John F. Kennedy, the then Vice President Nixon described the threat from China this way:

---

[4] Letter of transmittal from Secretary of State Acheson to President Truman, "United States Relations with China," Government Printing Office, 1949, p. XVI.

Now what do the Chinese Communists want?

They don't want just Quemoy and Matsu. They don't want just Formosa. They want the world.[5]

This distorted and mistaken view of China led directly to the McCarthy era which after a quarter of a century still afflicts American foreign policy. United States relations with China today are on a plateau, reached more than three years ago with the opening of diplomatic liaison offices in Peking and Washington. President Ford has repeatedly stated that the United States is determined "to complete the normalization of relations with the People's Republic of China on the basis of the Shanghai Communique,"[6] However, steps to do so have been taken with great reluctance. In my judgment, there has been a policy of avoidance. With the principal antagonists in the Chinese civil war now gone, it would seem to be a most propitious time to wipe the slate clean, to fulfill the promise of the Shanghai Communique by completing the process of normalizing relations with the People's Republic of China.

A. TAIWAN: UNTYING THE GORDIAN KNOT

"Those who cannot remember the past are condemned to repeat it," George Santayana wrote. That is especially pertinent to the position in which the United States finds itself concerning the normalization of relations with the People's Republic of China. An understanding of how United States policy came to be what it is today is essential to finding a solution to the current problem. There is only one obstacle to normalization. It derives from the events of 1949 when the forces led by Mao Tse-tung drove Chiang Kai-shek from the Mainland to the offshore island of Taiwan.[7] In the final years of that civil war the United States poured $2 billion of aid into a doomed cause. It was an intervention in China's civil war and it persists today through continuing U.S. recognition of the Republic of China on Taiwan, through the furnishing of that government with military advice and arms, through the conduct of joint maneuvers with its armed forces, and through many ties between America and the Nationalist government which are designed to preserve Taiwan as an entity separate from the Chinese mainland.

President Truman announced in early 1950 that the United States would "not provide military aid or advice to Chinese forces on Formosa" or "pursue a course which will lead to involvement in the civil conflict in China."[8] That policy was reversed six months later, following the outbreak of war in Korea, when President Truman ordered the U.S. Seventh Fleet to prevent a Chinese Communist attack on Taiwan and to stop Nationalist attacks against the Mainland. Intervention by Chinese forces in Korea in November locked in American support of the Nationalist regime. In his 1953 inaugural address President Eisenhower "unleashed" Chiang Kai-shek's forces, stating

---

[5] Television debate with John F. Kennedy, October 10, 1960.
[6] Speech at the University of Hawaii, Honolulu, Hawaii, December 7, 1975. See also President Ford's letters of April 11, 1975 and September 9, 1976, congratulating Hua Kuo-feng on his being named Premier of the People's Republic of China and of condolences on the death of Mao Tse-tung, respectively.
[7] Called Formosa by the Japanese who governed the island from 1895–1945 after being ceded the island in the Treaty of Shimonoseki which ended the Sino-Japanese war.
[8] Press Conference, January 5, 1950.

that the U.S. Seventh Fleet would no longer be "employed to shield Communist China." [9] Shortly thereafter the Nationalists began heavy fortification of Quemoy, Matsu, and the Tachens, small islands which lie several miles off the Chinese Mainland.

In early 1955 forces of the People's Republic seized a small Nationalist held island near the Tachen group and began a bombardment of the Tachens. This action led President Eisenhower to ask Congress to approve the Formosa Resolution, which, in effect, was a blank check for the President to wage war to defend Formosa, the Pescadores, and other islands then in Nationalists hands. Secretary Dulles, in presenting the Eisenhower Administration's case to a joint session of the Senate Foreign Relations and Armed Services Committees, stressed that the defense of Formosa was important to the security of the United States and denied any intention to intervene in China's continuing civil war.

> We say that the Island of Formosa and the Pescadores is an area which is vital to the interests of the United States, and that we are going to do what we can to see that it remains in friendly hands. If we were not there, if there was no other interest in this situation except that of two Chinese regimes, probably it would be considered to be purely a civil war.

> It does concern far more than them. It concerns the United States, and once we are in the situation, then these legal things that the two Chinese regimes argue about become quite unimportant. . . .[10]

As presented by Dulles, the alternatives to defending Formosa by risking war with China was that ". . . . we will be driven out of this whole Asian area and will fall back to the United States. That is the choice we have got to face." [11] The blank check resolution presented by the Eisenhower Administration and supported by the Joint Chiefs of Staff as essential to protection of America's vital interests, passed both Houses of Congress by overwhelming margins. It was not until 1974, that the resoution was repealed by Congress.

Two weeks after passage of the Formosa Resolution the Senate approved a treaty with the Nationalist government pledging the United States to defend Formosa and the Pescadores, after being presented with the same national security rationale used to obtain approval of the resolution. Secretary Dulles, testifying for the treaty in executive session before the Foreign Relations Committee painted a bleak picture of what would happen if the treaty were not approved. "If we," he said to the Committee, "allow that island chain to be broken through the Communists taking Formosa, in my opinion, the entire island chain will inevitably go. Japan will surely be lost, you will have a combination of power there of Russia, China and Japan, which will be more, a far more, serious threat than anything we have ever envisaged in that part of the world before, and our own defensive position will have to be pulled back very close to the Pacific mainland." [12]

[9] State of the Union Address to Congress, February 2, 1953.
[10] Unpublished hearings before a joint meeting of the Senate Committee on Foreign Relations and Armed Services, January 24, 1955, pp. 68–69.
[11] Ibid, p. 138.
[12] Unpublished hearing before the Senate Committee on Foreign Relations, February 7, 1955, p. 45.

The Committee's report on the treaty adopted the national security rationale pressed by the Eisenhower Administration, stating that the treaty ". . . does no more than formalize a policy which our government has followed for several years, to maintain Formosa as an essential anchor of our western defense chain." [13]

Time has proven that the justification presented to Congress for the defense treaty with the Nationalist regime was based on a distorted view not only of America s long-range interests in the Far East but also of the nature of the People's Republic of China. America's security was not involved in the future of Taiwan. The specter of political consequences at home, not military probabilities abroad, were the prime factors in distorting United States policy toward the Chinese civil war and in subsequently consolidating the distortions.

Concerning the Taiwan question, the Shanghai Communique stated:

> The Chinese side reaffirmed its position: The Taiwan question is the crucial question obstructing the normalization of relations between China and the United States; the Government of the People's Republic of China is the sole legal government of China; Taiwan is a province of China which has long been returned to the motherland; the liberation of Taiwan is China's internal affair in which no other country has the right to interfere; and all U.S. forces and military installations must be withdrawn from Taiwan. The Chinese Government firmly opposes any activities which aim at the creation of "one China, one Taiwan," "one China, two governments," "two Chinas," an "independent Taiwan" or advocate that "the status of Taiwan remains to be determined."

> The U.S. side declared: *The United States acknowledges that all Chinese on either side of the Taiwan Strait maintain there is but one China and that Taiwan is part of China. The United States Government does not challenge that position.* It reaffirms its interest in a peaceful settlement of the Taiwan question by the Chinese themselves. With this prospect in mind, it affirms the ultimate objective of the withdrawal of all U.S. forces and military installations from Taiwan. In the meantime, it will progressively reduce its forces and military installations on Taiwan as the tension in the area diminishes." (Italics supplied).[14]

Although the number of U.S. military personnel has been reduced substantially since 1972, there are still some 2,000 American servicemen stationed on Taiwan, including a military advisory group. Only this year the remaining U.S. military advisors were withdrawn from Quemoy and Matsu, islands not covered by the security treaty. The Indochina war, the "tension in the area," to which the language in the Shanghai Communique referred, is long since over. The bulk of the remaining American forces on Taiwan are engaged in activities which, if Americans put themselves in Chinese shoes, would be considered intolerable, since the activities are carried out on China's territory.

---

[13] Senate Executive Report 2. 84th Congress, 1st Session, February 8, 1955.
[14] Weekly Compilation of Presidential Documents, February 28, 1972, p. 475.

United States military involvement with the Nationalist government through the supply of military equipment has accelerated since 1972, not lessened. By the end of the current fiscal year a total of some $1.1 billion in military equipment and materials will have been provided by the U.S. to the government on Taiwan since the Shanghai Communique was issued, $378 million of that on a grant or credit basis. Additional military sales of several hundred millions of dollars are being planned for the 1978 fiscal year.

Official stimulus to economic ties continues. It is "business as usual" with U.S. private investments still flowing in, many protected by U.S. government guarantees through the Overseas Development Investment Corporation. Authorizations of direct loans and guarantees by the U.S. Export-Import Bank to finance sales to Taiwan totaled $1.24 billion in the 1972–75 period. United States firms are engaged in a major program which will make Taiwan dependent on nuclear power for half of its energy requirements by the early 1980's. No government agency has received new policy directions concerning the adjustment of U.S. relations with Taiwan in the light of the Shanghai Communique.

China's position on Taiwan is the same as it has been since the signing of the Shanghai Communique. It expects the United States to sever diplomatic relations with Taiwan, terminate the defense treaty, and withdraw all military forces from the island. "Any one principle missing won't do", a Chinese official said to me.

The Chinese refer to the application of the so-called Japanese-formula as a basis for full implementation of the Shanghai Communique. Since 1972, when it severed relations with Taiwan and established diplomatic relations with Peking, Japan's trade with and investments in Taiwan continue at high levels. Japanese affairs relating to the island are looked after by a quasi-official office called the Japanese Interchange Association. Taiwan maintains a similar non-diplomatic office in Tokyo. Other countries having diplomatic relations with China operate in Taiwan under similar arrangements. So could, apparently, United States private economic and cultural ties with Taiwan. There is no give, however, on the principle which the Chinese see involved: Taiwan is a part of China and when and how it will be absorbed into the life of the mainland is an internal affair. "They deal in principle, gentlemen", one thoughtful American in Peking observed. The first message issued by the Chinese Communist Party and other leadership organs after Chairman Mao's death reiterated the principle: "We are determined to liberate Taiwan."

The answer to the Taiwan problem is not to be found in Peking but in Washington. It is a domestic problem for the United States. "If this issue is not resolved and is prolonged, the responsibility is not on our side but on yours," said one Chinese official. Another added: "The one who ties a knot must untie it."

In the public report of my 1974 trip to China I said:

> The fact that must be faced is that we cannot have it both ways. We cannot strengthen our ties with a claimant government of China on Taiwan and, at the same time, expect to advance a new relationship with the government of the People's Republic of China. The Shanghai Communique was

designed as a transitional arrangement; it did not predicate
an indefinite ambivalence in our China policy.[15]

Much of the ambiguity concerning the Taiwan problem seems
to stem from the hope that with sufficient delay, the problem will
go away. A device in this connection, is the insistence that China renounce the use of force in regard to Taiwan. As far back as 1955,
China was prepared to agree to a joint statement renouncing the *general* use of force to settle disputes with the U.S. but would not renounce
its use specifically against Taiwan.[16] To appreciate what is involved in
the renounciation of force question, the issue should be examined from
the Chinese perspective. As the Chinese see it, Taiwan is an integral
part of China and, under the Shanghai Communique, the United States
does not dispute this contention. While there is no reason to assume
that the final withdrawal of U.S. forces will lead to the use of force
against Taiwan by the mainland, there is also no reason to expect
China to formally renounce its possible use against what it regards as a
Chinese province. Indeed to do so would be to cast a doubt on the validity of its claim to sovereignty over the island.

Taiwan is a point of utmost sensitivity in China's new national consciousness. Together with certain border areas along the frontier with
the Soviet Union it is the last vestige of China's humiliation at the
hands of outside powers. Equivocation over the Taiwan problem has
continued far too long. Ambivalence has created a dangerous situation
and further delay could bring about serious long-term consequences
for American policy in the Pacific area. For more than six years we
pursued a war in Indochina in the name of an illusive, undefined "peace
with honor," a quest which resulted in tragic losses of American and
other lives. Now there are signs that the same chimera is creating a
similar situation concerning the resolution of the Taiwan problem.
Delay has created new pressures for retention of the status quo, even
in Japan. References are made to an "easy-way out" of a "two-Germ-
any's" formula.

Stagnation is the enemy of a sound, constructive foreign policy, and
indecision in policy-making about Taiwan is providing political im-
petus for pushing citizens into choosing sides. There is a strong hint
of a resurgence of the divisiveness of a quarter century ago that led
to the current policy dilemma. The internal problems of China in
the wake of Mao's departure could create conditions in both countries
where the mutual interests now sustaining the relationship will be
weakened. The delay, for example, may well strengthen the hand of
the elements in the Chinese leadership seeking to restore greater
comity with the Soviet Union even at the expense of the U.S. relationship. The failure to face up to the Taiwan issue will only make the inevitable decision more difficult, controversial, and divisive.

It should be borne in mind that if full diplomatic relations are
established with the People's Republic of China, the treaty with the
Republic of China will fall. There can hardly be a continuance of a
defense treaty with one faction in a civil war while formal relations are maintained with the successor. When Japan recognized the
People's Republic of China in 1972, its treaty of friendship with

---

[15] "China: A Quarter Century After the Founding of the People's Republic", report to
the Senate Committee on Foreign Relations, January 1975. p. 23.
[16] See Appendix C for the texts of the series of proposals and counterproposals during
these negotiations.

Taiwan automatically lapsed. So will the U.S.-Taiwan security treaty. It has been urged that the treaty issue be handled by serving one-year notice of our intention to terminate the treaty, a right reserved to each under article X. This course would only further confuse the principle at issue. If Taiwan is a part of China, as the concerned parties now agree, serving a one-year notice to terminate the treaty means only additional delay in reconciling our official diplomatic posture and our national policy.

There is also the argument that for the United States to disengage from a military commitment to the Republic of China will suggest a weakening of American resolve about other defense obligations abroad. Unless the national interest controls foreign policy rather than vice-versa, this nation will be placed in an increasingly soffocating straight jacket with the ratification of every treaty. Treaties are not forever. They are national commitments subject to adjustment in the light of changing international realities and clearer perception of the national interest. The treaty was based in great part on U.S. security needs against a Moscow-directed axis with Peking, which is now seen to be a distortion. Moreover, the government of Taiwan claims to represent the people on the mainland, but it does not. It has ruled the island of Taiwan by martial law since 1949 in order to continue the trappings of a government for the entire Chinese mainland. Only 86 of the 1,288 seats in the National Assembly of the Republic of China and 49 of the 436 seats in the Legislative Yuan are held by the Taiwanese.

Some observers warn that Taiwan may either declare its independence or turn to the Soviet Union if the United States severs its treaty relationship. These arguments ignore the fact that Taiwan's lifeblood, until it is absorbed into the economy of the Mainland at some time in the distant future, is continued trade with the United States and Japan. These are not realistic alternatives for Taiwan but in any event were some such improbable situation to develop, it would be a Chinese problem and not one for this nation.

Although it is unrealistic to expect that the Chinese government will renounce the use of force to regain control of Taiwan, there is reason to expect that the Chinese will not rush the process of absorbing Taiwan into the life of the mainland after the normalization of relations between China and the United States has been accomplished. As the Chinese see the problem, acceptance of the principle at stake and the practical incorporation of Taiwan into the People's Republic are two different matters. The Chinese are impatient with regard to unequivocal acceptance of the principle, which stands in the way of complete normalization of relations, a process initiated by the Shanghai communique. "I think we have been patient enough," one official put it, "we have waited for more than twenty-seven years now." Even impatience over principle, however, can be tempered by priorities. International "issues," for example, meaning largely problems concerning the Soviet Union, receive first attention. Insofar as Taiwan is concerned, timing does not appear to be a pressing problem. While the process of absorption is regarded as inevitable it may well take many years.

On the basis of my conversations in China, I believe that satisfactory arrangements can be worked out concerning the handling of our residual relations with Taiwan, as has been the case with Japan and other countries, which will safeguard legitimate interests of U.S. citizens in that island. Moreover, I am persuaded that the Chinese know full well that any unprovoked military action in the Western Pacific would be a seriously unsettling event in Asia which could set off grave repercussions in the United States and Japan, to say the least. It would undermine a basic element in present Chinese foreign policy toward the Soviet Union. The peaceful merging of Taiwan with the mainland, therefore, would seem to be the implicit practical element in working out diplomatic arrangements between the People's Republic and the United States.

Congressional action may be necessary to arrange for continuation of trade and related ties to Taiwan to accord with a U.S. version of the "Japanese formula". In the spirit of bi-partisanship which has marked support of U.S. China policy since the Shanghai Communique, Congress should be prepared to take such action, as the Senate did in 1971 in approving S. Con. Res. 38 giving ". . . . full support to the President (Nixon) in seeking the normalization of relations with the People's Republic of China." [17]

It is important that a dialogue begin without delay between the People's Republic and Taiwan. The Shanghai Communique states that America's goal is "a peaceful settlement of the Taiwan question by the Chinese themselves." Leaders of the People's Republic have repeatedly expressed their willingness to engage in peaceful relations with Taiwan and have made gestures to underscore the point. United States policy should do nothing to discourage the Taiwan government from responding in kind.

All of the NATO allies, not to speak of dozens of other nations including Japan, have recognized the reality that the People's Republic is the rightful sovereign of all China, at no loss of their prestige in the world. One wonders which among them would label as an "abandonment", a U.S. policy of the same kind. There is not likely to be official collaboration with China on matters involving stability in the Pacific, disarmament, or other major world issues as long as the present state of affairs exists. The world applauded Nixon's trip to Peking. Whether or not it applauds the completion of the journey he started, it is essential in this nation's interest, in my judgment, that we move promptly in that direction.

B. TRADE AND EXCHANGES

Despite the absence of formal diplomatic relations, trade and personal contacts between the United States and China continue at a nominal level. Through these media the two nations are getting to know one another after a gap in contact of more than two decades. China has neither opened its doors to consumer oriented trade nor to the entry of the countless Americans who are fascinated by the ancient myth of a mysterious Cathay. China's principle of self-reliance negates the former and a traditional disinterest in the outside world plus the absence of extensive tourist facilities does the same for the latter. The early expectations of many Americans of a new market of more than

[17] S. Con. Res. 38, 92nd Congress, 1st Session, passed the Senate by voice vote on August 2, 1971.

800–950 million customers and an exciting new international tourist attraction have now subsided to a more realistic understanding of the situation.

1. Trade

United States trade with China has plunged from the high level of $934 million in 1974, when China bought large amounts of American grain, soybeans, and cotton, to $462 million in 1975. The lop-sided seven-to-one balance in the United States' favor was reduced to a more reasonable ratio of less than two-to-one. Trade in 1976 will total about $400 million, with U.S. exports at $220 million and imports from China of $180 million. Data concerning bilateral trade for 1971–1976 are shown in the table below:

UNITED STATES-PEOPLE'S REPUBLIC OF CHINA TRADE 1971-76

[In millions of dollars]

	U.S. imports	U.S. exports	Total
Calendar year—			
1971	4.9	(¹)	4.9
1972	32.3	60.2	92.5
1973	63.7	689.1	752.8
1974	115.0	819.0	934.0
1975	158.3	303.8	462.1
1976 (January–June)	89.6	119.6	
1976 (total estimate)	180.0	220.0	400.0

¹ Nil.

Since 1974 there has been a significant change in the composition of U.S. exports to China. With the exception of cotton, China did not buy any appreciable quantities of American farm products in 1975 or thus far in 1976, reflecting the improved state of Chinese agriculture which has built up sizable grain reserves. For such imports as it requires, moreover, China has returned to reliance on traditional import suppliers, Australia, Canada and Argentina. The value of U.S. agricultural exports to the People's Republic dropped from $665 million in 1974 to $79 million in 1975. In 1975, 60 percent of U.S. exports were manufactured goods and technology, the range running the gamut of American industry with primary emphasis on high technology items and data.

U.S. imports of Chinese goods have increased steadily, but not spectacularly, from $5 million in 1971 to an estimated $180 million this year. Last year tin was the major import, making up nearly 30 percent of the total value. A great variety of goods have come into the United States, many in small quantities. Chinoiserie, apparently, holds the public fancy.

American businessmen and Chinese traders are fast learning each other's needs and problems. The prospect is for a steady, but unspectacular increase in trade, unless political relations again sour. Two lesser difficulties, the claims-asset problem and the lack of most-favored-nation treatment for Chinese goods, impede normalization of trade relations. No progress has been made on either since my 1974 visit to China.

During the Korean war $76.5 million in Chinese assets in the United States, primarily bank deposits, were frozen by U.S. Government action. On the other hand, the Foreign Claims Settlement Commission has on file claims totaling $196.9 million by U.S. citizens against China. The majority are for small amounts, only nine are for more than $1 million. As long as this dispute continues direct banking, shipping, or any other activity which would result in Chinese-owned assets being present in the United States are not feasible. Any Chinese property in the United States, including ships, planes, or even a trade exhibit, is subject to being attached by a claimant against the country. The ten Boeing 707s sold to China cannot land at a U.S. airport, and China flag vessels cannot call at our ports to pick up goods American exporters have sold to the country. All financing of trade transactions have to be carried out through branches of third country banks in the United States. Another serious immediate consequence is that there cannot be an exchange of trade exhibits, which handicaps trade in both directions.

China's goods are not extended most-favored-nation tariff treatment by the United States. "Most-favored-nation" is a misnomer. It is not a favor; it is the normal basis of trade between nations of the world. Of the many nations with which this nation carried on trade last year only 15 did not receive this type of tariff treatment. Under the 1974 Trade Act, most-favored-nation treatment can now be accorded to China as well as certain other Communist countries, after a bilateral trade agreement is concluded and various conditions are met, including approval of the trade agreements by Congress. As long as this discrimination against China exists, importers must pay about four or five times the duties on Chinese imports that would apply to goods brought in from most other nations. It has been estimated that if Chinese goods received MFN treatment, imports from China would increase by as much as twenty percent. A basic trade agreement, moreover, would cover matters such as arrangements for settling disputes, patent and trademark protection, and trade promotion activities.

Agreement in principle was reached on the claims assets problem in 1973, but that question has not been pursued nor do the Chinese appear interested in moving forward on a trade agreement until the matter of diplomatic status has been settled.

2. Exchanges

The mutual learning process through exchanges of persons is proceeding satisfactorily although, as with trade, the balance is in the United States' favor. Approximately 12,000 Americans have visited China since the Shanghai Communique but as of November 1976 only 932 Chinese have come to the United States. Of the Americans going to China, only about five percent went through government facilitated exchanges, which, except for costs of international travel, are financed by the host government.

In the "facilitated" category, the United States has sent to China visitors such as most Congressional groups, state governors, scholars, sports teams and cultural groups. China has sent groups of technical experts, athletes, and performing artists, such as the Shenyang Acrobatic and the Wushu troupes. About half of the participants from both countries in the government-to-government exchanges have been members of sports teams or performing arts groups. Significantly, the exchange of political leaders has been a one-way street. China will not send officials here so long as the United States recognizes the government on Taiwan.

The Taiwan problem inevitably gives rise to friction in the official exchanges. In 1975, the planned visit by a Chinese performing arts group was cancelled because a song was added to the approved program selections which contained the lyrics "we must liberate Taiwan." Later in that year the Chinese objected to the presence of the Mayor of San Juan, Puerto Rico, on a list of U.S. mayors scheduled to visit China and the trip was cancelled. Ostensibly the objection was in line with Chinese support for a UN resolution favoring independence for Puerto Rico, but it may well have also been a tit for the earlier tat over the U.S. objection to the program selected by their performing arts troupe.

Most Americans have traveled to China not as official visitors but under private arrangements, either on their own or through membership in an organization. The U.S.-China Friendship Association, with branches operating in some 70 American cities, has sent many groups of interested Americans to China. It is not known, exactly, how many Americans have gone to China through unofficial channels, but probably the majority are Chinese-Americans, encouraged by China to make return visits to the land of their forebears. I visited in south Quangdong (Kwangtung) Province which is the place of ancestry for a large number of Chinese in the United States. In the village of Taishan, I found a large new hotel for overseas Chinese and a second, more modern hotel under construction. The private visits to China are essentially a one-way street. Only several hundred Chinese have come to the United States on this basis, mostly technicians coming over for training in the use of American equipment and technology, as was the case following the sale of 707s by Boeing and of fertilizer plants by the M. K. Kellog Co. Some Chinese have also come to visit relatives living in the United States.

As to tourism, the outlook is unchanged since my visit in 1974. Other than for visits by overseas Chinese, I did not detect any interest by Chinese officials in opening their country to large numbers of American tourists. In turn, the Chinese show little curiosity about the outside world. A usual justification for large-scale tourism is to earn foreign exchange. As indicated, Chinese facilities for handling tourists are still severely limited by a lack of hotel accommodations, interpreters, automobiles, and other amenities for international travelers. I saw no evidence anywhere in my travels of new tourist-type hotels being constructed or of any newly opened. The situation regarding American newsmen is also unchanged. Newsmen continue to be admitted as individuals but the Chinese position that permanent American news bureaus will not be allowed until after full restoration of diplomatic relations remains.

III. Chairman Mao Tse–tung's Legacy

It is difficult for one who had not personally seen the misery, sorrow, and degradation of life in old China, as I did as a U.S. Marine in the early 1920's and twice as a Congressman in the 1940's, to understand the significance of Mao Tse-tung to the Chinese people. To restore China's pride as a nation was one of Mao's major goals. Under his leadership, there has come into being for the first time in modern history a Chinese state under which the basic needs of the Chinese people—food, clothing, shelter, and health care—are met. In line with that fundamental achievement, the transformation of China into a modern industrial nation has been set in motion.

Although still a poor country by U.S. measure, China is well on the way to achieving a place of prestige in the world community. One hundred and ten nations have diplomatic relations with the People's Republic of China. Only twenty-six still recognize the Republic of China.[18] The United States is the only major nation which still maintains formal diplomatic ties with the Republic of China on Taiwan rather than with the Government in Peking. China is looked up to by many nations in the so-called Third World as an example of what can be achieved by self-reliance and independence.

As to Mao's social goals, the basic needs of the people, as noted, have been met. Food and clothing supplies are ample and low in price, housing is adequate, though primitive by our standards, particularly in remote rural areas. Health care is available to all. Bringing social benefits to the people—quantity—now has priority over quality, a Chinese leader told me. Quality, he said, will come in time. Relativity, *in the Chinese context,* is the key. I remember quite well that in the American depression a generation ago, when practically everyone in a still largely rural America was poor, one did not feel poor relative to his neighbors. Compared with the past, said a local leader in Shih Ho-tsu, a new city in remote Xinjiang (Sinkiang), the Chinese people are doing well. "Our situation is excellent," he put it simply.

Under the social system molded by Mao, the stress is on service. The heroes are those who work to get rid of the dry-rot in traditional social order and who contribute unselfishly to the long-range goal of improving the community, whether it be the commune, the factory or the nation. My observations, strongly suggest that the Chinese people have been imbued with the precept that there is a direct link between personal conduct and national goals. "Americans," one Chinese said, "may have put the first man on the moon but China will be the first to create a new man." "Serve the people" is not merely a slogan, it is a way of life reaching into the most remote parts of China. As with other aspects of Mao's doctrines, the principle has strong roots in Chinese tradition.

Stress is now placed on the "three-in-one" approach to leadership, combining the old, the middle-aged and the young. Another principle, "making the past serve the present," was exemplified by the preservation of several sand dunes in the Turpan (Turfan) depression. In an area where since 1964 hundreds of sand dunes had been leveled, turned into productive farm land, and stabilized by the planting of massive windbreaks, a few dunes had been retained, not only to show coming generations how bad the past used to be, but also to serve as a local spa for the treatment of arthritis.

From Shanghai in the East to Urumqi (Urumchi) in the West, from Beijing (Peking) in the North to Taishan in the South, wherever I visited there were impressive examples of efforts by individuals and groups working toward common goals. Material incentives are present

---

[18] See appendix D for lists of the countries recognizing each.

but they appear to be of less significance than the desire to achieve in terms of group objectives. Study sessions in factories and communes serve as an important link between every day conduct or performance on the job and national goals.

One of Mao's most important legacies is the doctrine of "self-reliance," a principle applied at every level of the government and to the international scene as well. The emphasis on local initiative carried out under basic policy guidance from the central government, called "walking on two legs," has been a key factor in the development of China's economy. Again, there are historical as well as practical roots for the stress on self-reliance. The Chinese are acutely sensitive to past humiliations suffered at the hands of outsiders culminating in the Soviet withdrawal of aid and technicians in 1960. This event led to a determined effort to minimize China's dependence on foreign sources for modernization and to apply this principle throughout every layer of government. "Rely mainly on our own efforts," Mao wrote, "while making external assistance subsidiary, break down blind faith, go in for industry, agriculture and technical and cultural revolutions independently, do away with slavishness. . . ."

Adherence to the doctrine of self-reliance has insulated China's economy from the vicissitudes of the world's economy to a degree not found in any other major nation. One recent example of self-reliance at work, was China's refusal to accept offers of outside aid after the devastating earthquake at Tangshan last August. The Chinese depend on the outside world for few raw materials, and with vast unexploited mineral and other resources, may eventually be completely self-sufficient. A prime benefit from self-reliance is that China, with its industry dispersed throughout the country, is in an excellent position to defend itself from outside attack. Decentralization of industry is being carried out both for practical and for strategic reasons.

From the production team of the commune to the national level, self-reliance is pursued religiously. The old Chinese tradition of emulation, following the good example set by the leader, is an important element in making the system work. In every commune visited there was a recital of the local unit's determination to "learn from Tachai," a model brigade of a commune which has achieved remarkable results in creating new productive land out of barren hillsides in Shansi Province. In the smallest and the largest factories, there was a dedication to "learning from Taching," a major oil refinery whose success is largely due to the initiative and ingenuity of the refinery workers.

At each level there are model factories and communes, not to impress foreign visitors since there are few, but to spur other local units to greater efforts. In the Xinjiang (Sinkiang) region, for example, there are 1,233 model farm units based on Tachai and 182 model factories for learning from Taching. The Hua-hsi Brigade, near Wuxi (Wu-shi) in Jiangsu (Kiangsu) Province, which I visited was a largely self-sufficient model brigade. It had achieved remarkable results in irrigation and in rationalizing use of its land by consolidation and leveling so that many of the farm operations could be mechanized. In Taishan County in Guangdong (Kwangtung) Province, I visited a small tractor factory which originally was a farm machinery repair shop. Last year it began producing 60 and 24 horsepower tractors using machines made primarily by its own workers in shops which they had constructed. It will turn out 200 tractors this year and plans to increase production to 3,000 units by 1980.

The Xinjiang (Sinkiang) region provides another example of self-reliance in operation at the provincial level. Until 1949, Xinjiang was a vast, thinly populated land of five million people scattered over a few oases and settlements, eking out a subsistence through primitive farming and animal husbandry. Today its population of eleven million work in factories or on well-managed farms, many of them mechanized. It is building a strong industrial base to exploit the area's vast natural resources, with plants already turning out steel and iron, petrochemicals, paper, textiles and other products.

It is also a province of significant geopolitical importance. The 3,000 miles of borders on five countries includes a long frontier with the Soviet Union that has been closed since 1962. Many Han Chinese have come into the region from the coastal areas in recent years but unlike past migrations, the rapid economic progress and an enlightened minorities policy has permitted their absorption without undue friction. Similar progress is being made in other remote parts of China, creating a more unified nation, while retaining the stress on local initiative.

An interesting aspect of the emulation approach to leadership is the fact that it has not resulted in competition between units. In no place visited did I hear any comparison between the brigade, the factory, or the province and a comparable unit. Competition is not intramural, it is with past performance. This attitude extends to the international scene as well. There is no indication that China is interested in engaging in competitive races with the outside world. Its self-confidence to date is free of arrogance.

Mao Tse-tung set out to create a unified China where traditional social and economic differences between classes, city and country, industry and agriculture, and mental and manual labor were eliminated. The meaningfulness of the task to the overall goal is stressed, not compensation. There are wage differentials but they are minimal. The average factory worker in Shanghai, for example, makes approximately $25–30 a month; the chief brain surgeon in a major local hospital in the same city makes $40 a month.

The local commune or factory party cadre, the managers in China's society, are expected to work closely with the peasants and workers. Bureaucrats are assigned to do manual labor periodically. This policy is put in practice most widely through the "May 7th schools," where cadre from governmental units at all levels combine farming with political study for a period of as long as a year. Attending such a school is not punishment but a normal part of training and discipline. "It chases away bureaucratic airs and teaches humility," one sophisticated Chinese bureaucrat said. Indeed, the techniques for keeping bureaucrats in touch with the grass roots may seem unusual to Americans, but the basic concept is hardly inimical to the preservation of a democratic society.

More than 12 million of China's middle school graduates, called "educated youths" have been sent from the cities to settle in remote or mountainous regions. The object is to carry out a two-way educational process, the young people pass on to the peasants any formal learning they have that can be applied to local problems. In turn, the young acquire basic skills and practical knowledge from the peasants. How well this system will work out in the long run remains to be seen, although both the young people and local leaders with whom I discussed the matter describe the results to date in glowing terms.

The legacy of ideas left by Chairman Mao will continue to be felt not only in China but throughout the world for decades to come. China does not project its influence abroad by military means; it has no troops outside its borders. Rather it does so through the projection of a cohesive culture and a coherent, viable society with great meaning for many nations of the world. China is self-confident and self-sufficient, able to take the long view of history. How China uses the tremendous power it is likely to possess a generation from now will be one of the most important factors in the world situation.

In the Shanghai Communique the United States and China agreed that five principles should guide relations between states: ". . . respect for the sovereignty and territorial integrity of all states, non-aggression against other states, non-interference in the affairs of other states, equality and mutual benefit, and peaceful co-existence." As a prescription for conduct between nations, the formula is not controversial. Problems arise, however, in the application of these principles to specific situations. The Chinese Communist Party is firmly committed to the belief that revolution is the means of bringing about basic social change in any country. China also takes the position that party and state actions are separate matters.

China's basic foreign policy objective is national security. It has a 2,600 mile border with the Soviet Union, a border which has been the source of much conflict over the centuries. In addition, seemingly of greater current importance to China, are ideological differences which exacerbate the traditional animosity. The Chinese are confident of their ability to meet any attack from the Soviet Union. A leader in the border area said to me: "We have no fear of them and are prepared. We will oppose a war of aggresion. Justice will be on our side and we are bound to triumph."

The resumption of friendly Sino-U.S. contact stems at least in part from the Sino-Soviet dispute. Absent a settlement o fthe Taiwan issue, this expediency sustains the U.S.-China relationship. Mao's legacy of ideological animosity to the Soviet Union, at least for the present, will also be a restraining influence on Chinese accommodation with the Soviet Union. There are indications, however, that steps may be taken to settle the disputes and return Sino-Soviet relations to a more normal state of affairs. A thaw is possible and when it comes it is imperative that our relations with China be in good repair.

Nationalism is a driving force in China. Mao's stress was not on projecting China's influence externally, but on restoring China's traditional role as a model society to be emulated by other nations. China remains pre-occupied with internal problems and that is likely to continue for the foreseeable future. China rejects superpower status, associating itself with the developing countries. What it shows to the Third World is an alternative to becoming tied to either of the superpowers and a model for the effective handling of development problems on a national basis. Chinese leaders deny any suggestion that they are the leader of the Third World, saying that such a role would violate China's principle of "never seeking hegemony." By putting agriculture first, China has succeeded in feeding its vast population without outside aid. This accomplishment has not gone unnoticed by the food-poor nations of the world. There can be little doubt that China's example will be of growing significance in the years ahead in an international community whose attention is increasingly concentrated on problems of resource allocation and social development.

Mao's goal for China, stated through Chou En-lai, was to build a comprehensive, independent industrial and economic system by 1980 and, in the second stage, to modernize its economy so that by the end of the century China's "economy will be advancing in the front ranks of the world." [19] On the basis of my observations in three visits over the last four and a half years, I believe that China is well on its way toward achieving its initial goal. It has solved the food problem and has made remarkable strides in population control. The standard of living, although meager by our standards, is constantly improving. Human muscle power is still more the rule than the exception in much of China's day-to-day development. But China is not a backward nation. It has capitalized on the ingenuity of the Chinese people and is proceeding on the thesis that nations, as well as humans, must learn to crawl before they can walk. What is of significance is that China has growing self-confidence in its capacity to leap-frog to the status of a modern industrial state. "Even if the sky should fall down," goes a Shanghai worker's slogan, "we will shoulder it."

There are problems ahead for China to be sure. The enormity of its problems, one Chinese bureaucrat said, could be appreciated from the simple fact that if each person ate another spoonful of rice a day, it would take an additional one million tons of rice each year to meet the new demand. Maintaining the revolution by avoiding the growth of elitism within the party bureaucracy is likely to be a continuing problem. Keeping the young, who have no personal memories of the "bad old days," filled with zeal may be another. There are also centrifugal forces at work between the provinces and the central government, between the army and elements in the party, between north and south, and between the old and the young. There is also the danger that human greed will re-surface in Mao's new man as the Chinese reach the stage where larger amounts of discretionary income are available. Notwithstanding these potential difficulties, Mao's precepts of self-reliance, serve-the-people, and his goal of abolishing basic social inequalities are likely to guide the country's leadership, whatever its make-up, for the foreseeable future.

Mao Tse-tung was one of the political giants of this age. He probably had a direct, personal, and positive impact on the lives of more people than any man in modern history. From a prostrate and divided country, under his leadership has emerged a unified nation of confident, self-reliant people whose pride in the past has been restored and who have a vision of a bright future. By any measure, China is a nation which must be increasingly reckoned with by the United States and the world. China has overcome vast obstacles in the short span of twenty-seven years. It is now in a position where, with effective leadership, its rate of progress can accelerate rapidly. By the turn of the century, China could be a giant, not only in human and natural resources, but also in its capacity to influence the world.

[19] See Appendix E for Premier Chou En-lai's speech of January 13, 1975, summarizing China's policy and objectives.

IV. Observations on the Current Scene in China

A. AGRICULTURE

China's economy is keyed to agriculture. It has the largest number of people and livestock to feed in the world. It leads in the production of rice, hogs (one-third of world's total) and poultry, and ranks second or third in wheat, corn, soybeans, cotton, sheep, horses and eggs. China's agricultural problem can be perceived in the stark statistics of its arable land. It is aiming to feed its 800–950 million people in a country whose arable land totals only about 265,000,000 acres. That figure compares with 435,000,000 acres in the United States with only one-fourth as many people to feed. Even India, with considerably less people, has about one-third more arable land.

As a matter of national policy, agriculture is the "foundation" of the economy. Some 80 percent of China's population lives in the countryside and agriculture contributes about 70 percent of the raw materials for China's light industry, which has priority after agriculture in development policy. All inhabited areas outside of cities and towns, except for a small percentage taken up by state farms, are divided into some 50,000 communes. Communes vary in population from 10,000 to 80,000 and are divided into production brigades which are subdivided into production teams. This smallest working unit consists of about 30 to 40 households, totaling 150 to 200 people, which is responsible for farming about 50 acres. A brigade might embrace five to ten production teams living in one or more villages. The commune today is primarily an administrative unit, day-to-day economic and social life centers in the production brigades and teams.

In an area like Xinjiang (Sinkiang), a border land with difficult climate, soil and terrain conditions, the approach to agricultural organization varies from the norm. Whereas the commune structure, essentially a cooperative system based on people who already inhabited the area, is typical of most of China, in Xinjiang (Sinkiang) there are also state farms which operate on a different principle. State farms account for 35 percent of the cultivated land and produce more than one-fourth of the area's grain. After 1949, units of the People's Liberation Army (PLA) were sent into the area to establish farms on what had been barren land. The PLA enterprises have evolved into state farms and the soldiers have long since been demobilized. New people, primarily Han, migrating to the province have swollen the population of the state farms. The Number 143 State Farm in Shih Hotzu, which I visited, has expanded many times since it was established. In the beginning it consisted of about 1,000 people on 650–800 acres of land. It now has 40,000 people on 34,000 acres. Half of its population is made up of young children and students. The birth rate was once twenty per thousand, but is said to be declining as a result of efforts to promote family planning. Only part of the population increase on the farm is attributable to the high birth rate; much stems from the influx of Han youth from outside the province.

On state farms such as Number 143, the State is the owner and employer, whereas on communes the land is owned in common by the residents with their income coming primarily from sale of the produce of the commune to the state. One significance of the state farms, which control 5–10 percent of China's agricultural land, is that they are vehicles for developing previously unproductive land in remote regions, thus providing a livelihood for new settlers. On the Number 143 State Farm the workers earn wages averaging about 50 yuan ($25) a month. They have no private plots as on communes. They construct their own houses, make their own implements, and provide for many of their other needs. Only a single crop a year can be cultivated there—maize, wheat, cotton and sugar beets. Pigs, sheep and poultry are also raised. Food processing is an important adjunct of agriculture.

China has been able to push its grain harvests upwards each year by stressing a national policy of "taking grain as the key link." In application, this means, first, improving and expanding, by "rural capital construction", China's limited arable area. What is involved is leveling, terracing, and reclaiming millions of acres of previously unproductive land every year, and improving the irrigation and drainage of cultivated land. This requires the back-breaking toil of a hundred million peasants or more each winter season. I saw much leveling and terracing going on as I traveled through the countryside. It is work that obviously could be performed more expeditiously and on a larger scale if more earth-moving machinery were available. The magnitude of the largely human-labor effort, however, can be seen in the achievements registered under the Fourth Five-Year Plan (1971–1975). Over 80 million acres of land were leveled, a process essential to mechanization and use of irrigation. Twenty million acres were brought under new or improved irrigation, about 17 million acres were protected from waterlogging and about eight million acres were terraced.

Multiple cropping is being increased as a means of expanding output. New strains of grains with shorter growing seasons and higher yields are being developed. In Jiangsu (Kiangsu) province a typical sequence is two crops of rice followed by one of wheat. The Yunghe Production Team of the Tuanfen People's Commune in Taishan County, Guangdong (Kwangtung) province, which I visited, regularly produces three crops and now gets four in several of its fields.

With agriculture the top priority, industry directs its efforts to supporting it by producing machinery, fertilizer, and insecticides. To achieve mechanization "in the main" by 1980, as called for by now party Chairman and Premier Hua Kuo-feng [20] in the fall of 1975, industrial inputs on a vastly increased scale will be necessary. I saw many impressive examples of local efforts to meet this goal.

Turpan (Turfan) County in the Turpan Depression in Xinjiang (Sinkiang) Province is an unusual example of the massive effort to improve agricultural production. The Turpan Depression drops to more than 500 feet below sea level. It is a place of intense heat in summer, fierce winds, and virtually no rainfall. It was once known as the "land of fire." For the summer months the temperature averages about 104 degrees and often goes as high as 116 degrees. The ground surface temperature reaches 160 degrees. Rainfall averages one-third of an inch per year, but the annual evaporation rate is about 75 inches. The winds are so strong that in the past crops have simply blown away. In this inhospitable environment of aridity, sand, and wind, self-help programs have been organized to fight the sand dunes and the

---

[20] Hua was then a Vice-Premier and a member of the Politburo.

wind, and to create a prosperous agriculture and new industries. The leader of the Forward Brigade of the Five Star People's Commune described how windbreaks were built to protect the land from wind and drifting sand. Windbelts composed of 10 rows of poplar trees in five tracks with irrigation ditches between have been planted under a long-term program started in 1964. The main wind barrier was three kilometers long with about 400,000 trees. Two other similar belts of trees have been completed and two more are planned by the brigade. Within the belt fruit trees and grapevines have been planted. In addition, there are lesser belts around individual plots of cultivated land. Altogether in the Turpan area some 850 miles of windbreaks have been established.

The key to local agricultural success has been the increased availability of water. This has been brought about by three methods. First, the people of Turpan built 400 miles of canals to tap the waters of distant snow-covered mountains. Second, they dug some 600 traditional wells. The third method is by what is called the "Karez Well," a system consisting of a series of wells sunk to an underground water flow which starts at the foot of the distant snow covered mountains with the wells decreasing in depth as they approach the agricultural area. This ingenious system is designed to keep the ground water from being dissipated in the sand. There are about 500 Karez Wells in Turpan County, all interconnected with the canals.

Turpan County covers 4,000 square miles, with 50,000 acres of cultivated land. The population of 139,000 lives in ten towns, seven communes, and one state farm. Until about ten or so years ago, the sand drift in Turpan was so relentless that houses and villages were sometimes buried and many people forced to move from their homes. The drifts have now been blocked. Over 1,000 sand dunes have been leveled and turned into productive farm land. The sand drifts and dunes have been controlled by windbreaks, flushing, manual spreading and tractors. Sand has been carried away to improve barren land and the composition of the soil elsewhere.

Before 1949 "the people led a miserable life," a local leader said. Now the area under cultivation has doubled and crop yields have greatly increased. In the past grain was short; now the county sends grain to the state. The living standard, we were told, has improved so that the production teams now have large grain reserves, money in the bank, and the people "wear woolens and silks and have bicycles, radios and watches."

In 1964 Chairman Mao declared, "In agriculture, learn from Tachai." Tachai is a production brigade in Shanxi (Shansi) province which achieved an impressive record in turning barren, mountainous terrain into productive land while overcoming difficult obstacles of morale and weather. "Learn from Tachai," is a constant refrain in the countryside throughout China, with Tachai held up as a model for all communes, brigades and teams to emulate. At the 1975 agricultural conference, the then Vice-Premier Hua Kuo-feng set forth as a goal that more than one-third of China's counties should become "Tachai-type" counties by 1980. More than 300 counties had already so distinguished themselves, he declared, but at least 100 more "Tachai-type" counties should be added annually for the next five years.

An example of "learning from Tachai" is the Hua-hsi Brigade in Jiangsu (Kiangsu) province. This advanced brigade lives in a neatly laid out village. It contains 1026 persons in 285 households, who farm 140 acres. Be.ore 1949 the area consisted of many small, unproductive, plots of irregular land. Grain production was about 1500 pounds an acre. In 1964 the brigade adopted a fifteen-year development plan to increase production to 6 tons an acre. The goal was achieved in eight years. In 1975 the two crops of rice and one of wheat grown by this brigade amounted to about 7.5 tons an acre. The increase was made possible primarily by the consolidation and leveling of 1300 small uneven plots into 400 larger plots, and by increased mechanization.

The living standards of the brigade members have risen substantially during this period. Average annual income is now more than double that of 1963 and every family has money in the bank and grain reserves. The peasants have moved into new homes, including some new two-story houses which, although modest by American standards, are markedly more comfortable than the older housing. The brigade has preserved one house and a small plot of land from the old days to make young people understand how the present compares with the past. The brigade provides services such as a tailor, barber, bathhouse, shoe repair and a variety of small stores. Private plots are farmed collectively and fresh vegetables delivered daily to each household. There are free primary and middle schools for the children as well as a nursery and a kindergarten. Several barefoot doctors operate a small clinic. The economy of Hua-hsi has been diversified. Earlier the brigade concentrated on growing rice. Now it has orchards, fisheries and raises stock animals. Half of the brigade's income comes from occupations other than raising grain. The Hua-hsi Brigade is now proceeding under a second economic plan that seeks by the early 1980's to accomplish such goals as production of ten tons of grain an acre, diversification, complete mechanization in agricultural production, and the provision of a new, two-story dwelling to every household. The plan's success depends heavily on mechanization. On all farms I visited there was some degree of mechanization and plans for more. Mechanization can be applied to planting, plowing, harvesting, irrigation, grading, transportation and other operations such as the processing of food. How fast China can fabricate and put into fields the machines for these purposes depends on many factors. It depends on the competition for available iron and steel and on local factors affecting the production teams and brigades, including personal initiative, topography, soil conditions and finances.

Despite continuing advances in agricultural output, there is still rationing of grain, cooking oil and cotton goods. Mixtures of cotton and synthetic fibers are not subject to rationing. Replacement of cotton with synthetics is encouraged to release cotton acreage for other crops. Increased use of synthetics is also in harmony with China's rising petroleum output.

After centuries of stripping the forests, wood has been a scarce commodity in most parts of China for a long time. Concrete is used for many purposes where wood would normally be employed in the United States, for example, in electric poles, railroad ties and small boats. One of the most significant agricultural achievements since 1949 has been in tree-planting. Virtually everywhere there were immense plantings of trees, often in multiple rows, along the roads, rivers, canals, and irrigation ditches. While it was difficult to get comprehensive figures, I was told that in the city of Nanjing (Nanking) alone, for example, 26,000,000 trees had been planted since liberation. Afforestation programs have been included in national plans for agriculture for the past two decades and from my observations, it would seem that within a decade China may be able to satisfy completely its need for wood. In fact, paper and plywood have been significant exports during the past several years.

B. OTHER ASPECTS OF CHINA'S ECONOMY

"Take agriculture as the foundation and industry as the leading factor" sums up priorities for developing China's economy. Agriculture comes first, followed by light industry and, last, heavy industry. Light industry and agriculture are closely linked because two-thirds of the raw materials for light industry come from agriculture. Growth in the agricultural and light industrial sectors provides the basis for financing as well as the market for heavy industry, which in turn produces the machinery, transport and so on that sustain progress in agriculture and light industry.

The performance of the economy in 1975, the last year of the Fourth Five-Year Plan and the latest year for which generalizations can be made, advanced China another step toward immediate and future goals. Value of industrial production rose about ten percent over 1974, a year of lesser gains. Large increases were recorded in production of such items as radios, watches, bicycles, sewing machines, cameras, yarns and textiles. Judging by the goods observed in department and other stores in Urunqi (Urunchi), Beijing (Peking), Guangzhou (Canton), and Shanghai, there seem to be adequate supplies of these items for domestic consumption. Stores are well stocked and jammed with customers.

The emphasis placed on light industry over heavy industry has clearly helped to meet the needs and desires of the people. Light industries, moreover, include those that happen to harmonize with traditional skills of the Chinese and are capable of earning foreign exchange. During my visit I toured several small factories which illustrated the practical approach to China's industrial development. The August First Woolen Mill in Shih Ho-tzu in Xinjiang (Sinkiang) province, was established to process the wool from the sheep that are raised in the area. This factory was started in 1958 on a stretch of desert. With 53,000 spindles and 2,500 workers in seven workshops, it now turns out piece goods and yarns that are exported to ten countries, including some in Eastern Europe as well as Korea, Vietnam, Cuba, Kuwait and Hong Kong. I also toured the July First Cotton Textile Mill in Urumqi (Urumchi) in the same province. Although Xinjiang (Sinkiang) produced cotton in 1949, cloth and thread were then made only by hand. A PLA unit in Urumqi (Urumchi) started the mill which went into production in 1952. It now has 100,000 spindles and 8,300 workers.

Another example of local initiative is the small factory I observed in Hsinhui, Guangdong (Kwangtung) Province. The Artistic Palm Products Factory has capitalized on the palm tree which is native to Hsinhui. In 1958 local workers made the machines for processi~ the palm leaf and the factory now has 500 employees turning o` variety of products such as mats, fans, hats, curtains and bask

Still another example of light industry which has capitalized on an ancient Chinese skill and local resources is the Taishan Porcelain Factory also in Guangdong (Kwangtung) province. It produces chinaware and porcelain products for both domestic use and export. The factory was established during the "Greap Leap Forward" in 1958. No such industry had previously existed in Taishan County. It now produces about 20 different pottery products and forty percent of its annual production of 10 million pieces is exported. I saw saucers destined for Africa, bowls for Thailand and Malaysia and teapots for Southeast Asia. Small local factories like these, keyed to local needs and resources, can be seen throughout China. They constitute the basic foundation of China's industrial development efforts and are not only significant for internal consumption but are often foreign exchange earners.

Top priority is assigned to industry which aids in expanding agricultural production. The increase in production of large and walking tractors and farm related diesel engines, in 1975 over 1974, for example, was stated as 40%. The walking tractor is a versatile machine especially useful in rural areas in the present stage of China's development. It is a motorized, hand or foot guided machine that can accommodate an assortment of attachments, including wheeled carriers that convert it into a means of transport. I saw thousands on the streets and roads of China, filling a gap between large trucks and bicycles or push carts. The primary use of the machine, however, is in the fields. One can plow an acre of ground in an hour. From a small shop with 13 workers set up in 1956 to make hand tools such as hoes and sickles, the Farm Machinery Factory in Hsinhui County has developed into a factory with 750 workers that in 1975 turned out 7,500 "worker-peasant" Type Ten walking tractors and expects to produce 8,500 this year.

As China's economy develops it can be expected that heavy industry and energy will receive more attention. Indeed, a trend in this direction is already detectable. Capital construction in 1975 was up perhaps twenty percent over 1974, including for example, expansion in such industries as electric power, petroleum, coal, motor vehicle, fertilizer and sugar refining. An example of heavy industry which came to my attention was the Shanghai Electrical Machinery Plant in Minhang, a satellite city of 80,000 people in the Shanghai Municipality. The factory builds turbo-generators and electric motors. With 800 workers, it is one of a number of plants located in this Shanghai suburb. The Electrical Machinery Plant came to Minhang in 1951 with a couple of hundred workers. In 1954 it turned out a generator of 6000 KW, using a foreign design. Employing local engineering and design skills, the plant turned out successively larger generators until now it produces generators with ratings as high as 300,000 KW. Although many of the workers learned techniques and engineering skills through practice and study at the factory, it has engineers from universities in many parts of China and one received training in the United States. Production in this plant in 1975 was said to be eight-fold that of 1965. While generators of various capacity are produced, two or three each year are of the largest size, 300,000 KW. Presently programed is a 600,000 KW generator.

A weakness in China's development effort exists in the iron and steel industry. Output is increasing slowly, and imports are still necessary. In the early fifties China's production of crude steel was only a few million metric tons a year; in 1971, it was 21 million tons. After fluctuating, it increased to only 26 million metric tons in 1975. A further increase in capacity can be expected when new plants supplied by Japan and Germany come on the line in 1978.

Even in heavy industry, the stress remains on self-reliance. The Yangtze River Bridge at Nanjing (Nanking) is an example of advanced engineering and complex steel casting accomplished by Chinese technicians. It is both a railroad and highway span, a key transportation link between north and south China. The railway portion of the bridge is over 22,000 feet, with the span running more than a mile over the water. China had not previously made the special steel required in construction of the bridge and had contracted with the Soviet Union to supply it. When the break came with Moscow, China was thrown back on its own ingenuity. The Anshan Iron and Steel Works in North China came up with the required steel and the bridge opened on schedule in 1968. The economic importance of the bridge, although it is not the only bridge over the Yangtze, is shown by the traffic which it carriers. About 120 trains cross each day, compared with about 40 a day by the old ferry method.

During my recent visit, which carried me to distant parts of China, I observed that electricity had become available virtually everywhere. Even the humblest dwellings in rural areas had electric lines running in to them. During the quarter century of the existence of the People's Republic, China has become a major producer of energy—third in the world in coal production, sixth in natural gas and thirteenth in petroleum. Hydroelectric power is still a minor source.

The following table shows comparative growth.

CHINA: PRODUCTION OF PRIMARY ENERGY

	Total	Coal	Oil	Natural gas	Hydroelectric
	Million metric tons of coal equivalent				
1965	198	169	16	12	1
1970	306	233	43	28	2
1974	428	289	98	38	3
	Percent				
1965	100	85	8	6	1
1970	100	76	14	9	1
1974	100	67	23	9	1

China has large reserves of coal, with some in virtually every province. In the past the best deposits were in the North and Northeast and there was thought to be little elsewhere. In recent years the discovery of substantial deposits in the South has greatly improved national availability. Shortages in coal production within the past several years, have caused problems for the iron and steel industry, the railroads and fertilizer production. Coal production had been in a slump for several years, partly because of equipment and labor troubles but production gains were registered in 1975 with output at about 430 million metric tons, compared with almost 590 million metric tons in the United States. A national conference on coal was held in Beijing (Peking) in late 1975 at which a program for mechanization and the development of new capacity was unveiled. It will take several years, however, for this to bear fruit.

China's exploitation of its petroleum resources has resulted in rapid increases of its production in recent years. New fields have been discovered and oil fields have been more intensively worked. Production has been expanding at a rate of 20 percent a year and in 1975 was about 80 million metric tons. This compares with almost 420 million metric tons in the United States in the same year. Last year China publicized the development of offshore drilling capacity in shallow waters of the Gulf of Pohai. For reasons not altogether clear, the rate of increase in oil production diminished in 1976 and exports declined. Although China has relied to some extent on foreign equipment, it rejects foreign participation in the exploitation of its oil resources. At present there appears to be no intention to permit any foreign company to receive exploration, drilling or similar concessions. Processing capabilities lag behind petroleum output but this gap could be narrowed or eliminated when new refineries in eastern cities come into operation in the near future. As to the future, problems in stimulating coal production make it doubtful that the rate of increase in energy output can be maintained let alone accelerated. As a result, demand for energy may mount faster than the supply. Such a development would both affect petroleum exports and make hydroelectric power more attractive. Water power has been a minor source of energy and by its nature cannot become a major challenger of either coal or oil. Nevertheless, in mountainous China hydro power is a promising source.

I visited a hydroelectric system in the Kutou Mountains of Guangdong (Kwangtung) province. This enterprise was started in 1958 as an afforestation and tree farming project and beginning in 1970 a complex of reservoirs, water channels and power stations was added. The tree farms were expanded, fruit trees planted, and the reservoirs stocked with fish. The centerpiece of this complex is a system of ten reservoirs, dams, channels and hydrogenerator stations at descending levels of the mountains. The twenty "small-sized," as they were described, hydroelectric generators add up to a total capacity of only 7,000 KW. A plan is being put into effect, however, to expand the capacity of the generators to 10,000 KW but, judging by the volume of the water, and the length of descent, the potential is much higher. A principal significance of the system is that it was built from scratch by local labor. It was an impressive example of the doctrine of "self-reliance" in practice.

Recent figures for the first half of 1976 indicate that the Fifth Five-Year Plan (1976–1980) is off to a good start and is continuing the long-term growth trend. The gross value of industrial output was up 7 percent over the first half of 1975 and the machine building industry is reported to have fulfilled more than half of the 1976 production plan in the first half of the year. Coal, gas, and electric power were all up, but it is noteworthy that the increase in oil production in the first half slipped from the 20 percent level achieved in recent years to about ten percent. In certain industries the completion in 1976 of the first contingent of two billion dollars worth of imported plants and equipment under the Fourth Five-Year Plan will add to the capital base, particularly in the petroleum, chemical, and synthetic fiber industries.

Attaining success in the Fifth Five-Year Plan (1976–1980) is critical for advancing toward the mid-term goals of "independent" and "relatively comprehensive" development by the 1980's although the specific goals of that plan have not been disclosed. The political problems of the past year, the first year of that plan, undoubtedly absorbed an undue amount of the government's attention but reports at the end of October were that the government press has again stressed former Premier Chou's goal of modernizing the economy.

It seems that the question of how much priority industry will receive will depend on the progress made in agriculture. Progress in the later has been so rapid that a point could be approaching at which a decision to allocate higher priorities to industry might be taken. This could become one of the salient features of the Fifth Five-Year Plan.

C. FOREIGN TRADE

China's foreign trade is controlled by the Beijing (Peking) government and is not subject to decision by lesser authorities or by private individuals. Since it is so much an instrument of national policy, foreign trade is responsive to the political philosophies that compete within the party hierarchy.

The power of the principle of self-reliance in molding the economic effort of the Chinese people has been described earlier in this report. It is a particularly influencial principle in foreign trade policy. But self-reliance does not stand in the way of trade that can be conducted on a basis of "equality and mutual benefit", trade that does not lead to dependence on foreigners. A principle of China's trade practice is that economic aid and loans, other than normal supplier credits, should not be accepted from abroad. China is proud that it is in debt to no one and evidently it intends to maintain that course. The New China News Agency recently explained:

> We stand for independence and self-reliance. This does not mean we decline to study foreign experience, neither does it mean that we lock our door against the world and refuse to develop foreign trade or to introduce from abroad certain techniques and equipment really useful to China.

It is a matter of profiting from, and not becoming dependent on, foreign technology and equipment.

Commerce with other nations contributes only marginally to China's economy. Therefore, the debate between the "moderates" and "radicals" over how much stress to place on foreign technology, relates only to a marginal, but significant, component of the national economic structure. Briefly, the "moderates" favor increased trade with other countries to obtain the sophisticated technology and equipment China needs for development, while the "radicals," assigning greater weight to ideology, are reluctant to increase China's dependence on external sources and also fear that such trade relations would stimulate growth of a technically oriented bureaucracy remote from the people. The surge in China's trade since 1972 reflects the philosophy of the "moderates." The years 1973–1975 were marked by several notable develop-

ments—the orders for whole plants and machinery from abroad as a
spur to heavy industry, the mushrooming sales of petroleum, and the
incurring of a large deficit followed by efforts to bring trade once more
into balance. Self-reliance has remained a potent factor, however, so
that China has advanced technologically without a massive input of
foreign technology. Repeatedly in my travels I was told in factory
after factory how the workers had built their own machines, often
modeled on others, but in many cases improved by indigenous innova-
tions. Imported equipment makes up only a small portion of the machines in China's fields and factories. The qualitative input from foreign imports, however, could be of key significance in particular situations, such as in the case of the purchase of prototype plants and
advanced computers.

China's trade began a rapid expansion in 1973, increasing to $10 bil-
lion from $6 billion the previous year. In 1974 trade soared to nearly
$14 billion but the deficit also climbed from $170 million to $810 mil-
lion. The trade deficit was cut to $400 million in 1975, not by changing
the general pattern substantially—but by selling more to developed
countries and importing less from developing countries. In 1975 the
direction of trade shifted more towards Japan, Hong Kong (which
respectively rank one and two as China's trading partners), Western
Europe and Rumania, and away from the United States and Canada.
More than four-fifths of China's trade is now with non-Communist
countries, but trade with Communist nations provides China with a
substantial market for commodities, unsalable in the West, which can
be exchanged for industrial goods. Imports of agricultural products,
such as grains, cotton and soybeans, were reduced, because burgeoning
harvests have built up China's reserves. Imports of machinery and
plant equipment increased by 30 percent, mostly in fulfillment of whole
plant contracts made in 1973–1974. Contracts for entire plants, such as
petrochemical and metallurgical complexes, reached a peak of $1.2 bil-
lion in 1973, dropped to about $850 million in 1974 and to less than
$400 million in 1975. The policy of buying whole plants was justified
in the face of China's policy of self-reliance on the grounds that such
imports would in the long run advance that principle. China's 1975
exports increased over 1974. Although traditional exports, food, textiles, and handicrafts, receded somewhat because of the slack world
economy, China more than made up the difference with petroleum exports which rose to about one billion dollars. Visible trends in 1976
show some slackening of trade expansion, primarily because of a de-
crease in oil exports, but there could be some increase in traditional
Chinese exports due to improvement of the world's economy and more
effective promotion of exports.

Hong Kong is a special situation in China's external trade. In an
economic sense, British-governed Hong Kong is an outpost of China
and its principal contact with the capitalistic world. Hong Kong is a
prolific earner of foreign currency for the People's Republic. This
helps to explain why Peking shows no haste in reasserting sovereignty
over the British-ruled enclave. This city of 4.4 million pople, almost
all Chinese, is China's second largest trading partner, behind only
Japan. In 1975 China exports to Hong Kong totaled $1.4 billion dol-
lars while only five million dollars of goods were bought from the

colony. China's favorable balance with Hong Kong is almost twice its deficit with Japan.

Although China is philosophically opposed to foreign investment on its soil it has not hesitated to invest in Hong Kong. China, in a display of what has been called "commercialized communism," has made investments in a great variety of firms and enterprises in Hong Kong which bring a rich return, including banks, department stores, commercial agencies and distributors, manufacturing firms, warehouses, and insurance companies. Profits from these investments, borrowings from Beijing (Peking)-owned or controlled banks, and remittances to China by Chinese in Hong Kong amount to perhaps an additional 600 million dollars. Pragmatically, the foreign exchange which Hong Kong provides helps China to acquire the high technology and machines it needs from abroad to achieve the goals outlined by Premier Chou at the Fourth National Congress. In turn, Hong Kong with its millions of inhabitants would find it difficult, if not impossible, to exist without the food, fuel, textiles and even water that China supplies. The colony cannot be self sufficient nor can it easily shift to other suppliers. China derives a number of auxiliary benefits from the Hong Kong connection. For instance, Hong Kong serves as an important port for China which has a shortage of harbor facilities. It is a neutral site where businessmen from many different countries can make contact with the Chinese to explore matters of mutual interest. Hong Kong has channels of information about economic, financial and other world developments which are of value to somewhat isolated Chinese officials. Finally Hong Kong is, in a sense, a school for China's officials to learn worldwide trading and marketing techniques in a supply and demand environment. These techniques may be of increasing benefit as industrialization proceeds in China and it aspires to greater participation in world trade and finance.

D. EDUCATION—PRACTICAL AND IDEOLOGICAL

In China today education takes place on a mass scale. One-fifth of the population is in school at the primary, middle and university levels. Add to this the many millions who are in factory, vocational and other short-term training or are taking correspondence courses offered by the universities and other educational institutions and one can reasonably estimate that one-third to one-half of the Chinese people are engaged in full-time or part-time study of one kind or another. This is a far cry from the massive illiteracy of pre-1949 China.

China's educational system was drastically transformed during the Cultural Revolution. "Education," Chairman Mao declared, "must serve proletarian politics and be combined with productive labor." In the judgment of party leaders, students in the educational system had been isolated from the life and labor of the workers and peasants and were learning "by rote" subjects of social irrelevance. Graduates were thought to be incapable of assuming the tasks of China's socialist society and to constitute an intellectual elite out of touch with the working class. Changes were instituted to end those conditions by changing the educational process to give priority to "revolutionary" purposes.

At present, the normal sequence for study is five years of primary school followed by five years of middle school following which graduates go to work in factory or commune. But throughout there is much exposure to practical work experience. The reforms in education instituted during the cultural revolution are exemplified in the Teachers College at Nanjing (Nanking), which I visited. The cultural revolution brought about a change in the philosophy, curricula and administrative procedures of the school in order to conform with Chairman Mao's principle that "education must serve a proletarian purpose." The spirit of the political transformation of the system is evident in the new criteria for admission to the school. Previously acceptance for enrollment depended on graduation from middle school and receiving good marks in national entrance examinations. Now applicants must have at least two years of experience in factories or communes and be recommended by their local revolutionary committee. College officials asserted that priority is given to the "political consciousness" of the applicants as shown in their work. Under this policy, most enrollees are still middle school graduates, but some are not. In the interest of making the curriculum more practical (the earlier "theoretical" nature of education is condemned) the four-year curriculum was shortened to three and the students now spend three months of each year working in factories or communes. The principal subjects taught in the teachers college do not appear unusual—Chinese language, foreign languages, the art of teaching, political education, music, fine arts, mathematics, physics, chemistry, biology, and geography. It also conducts courses for factory workers and people in rural areas. About 3,000 students attend short courses and 4,000 take correspondence courses, in addition to the 2,400 regular students.

Training in primary and middle schools is tied to day-to-day life. Schools have a close relationship to work on farms and in factories and usually combine learning with practical experience. Military training is also stressed. A vivid example of this approach in practice was seen at the Number Five Municipal Primary School in Urumqi (Urumchi). One of the features of this school of 1,800 students was a small rug weaving operation in which the students obtained practical training and, in the process, earned some $20,000 annually for the school from sale of the rugs. Another feature was a rifle team of thirteen-year-old boys and girls who gave an impressive demonstration of marksmanship.

Several of the factories I visited had "July 21 Workers' Colleges." These are schools initiated by a 1968 directive of Chairman Mao designed to improve the technical knowledge and political consciousness of the workers. China needs many highly skilled technicians and, in the view of the government, these technicians should be imbued with a socialist, proletarian consciousness. Workers' Colleges are designed to fulfill these requirements. They are run by factories and aimed at training ordinary workers to become skilled technicians. The students, according to recent figures, now number almost eight hundred thousand in 15,000 such colleges. The courses range from several months to as long as three years, concentrating on engineering, physical sciences and mathematics. Other subjects such as liberal arts and medicine are also taught. Instructors are frequently workers from the factory, but sometimes engineers and technicians from other schools. The courses are tied closely to practical experience in the factory but also include a theoretical content. The graduates from these schools are significantly raising the standards of technology in China's factories and may well be breaking down distinctions between technicians and workers.

A special kind of school, intended for managers (cadre) in both governmental and non-governmental occupations, are "May Seventh" schools, initiated by a directive issued by Chairman Mao on May 7, 1966. The May Seventh school I visited was typical. Established to train cadres in the Eastern District (one of four municipal districts) of Beijing (Peking), it had 300 students drawn from government organizations, factories, hospitals, shops and schools. The purpose of the May Seventh school is mainly political, to indoctrinate leaders with socialist ideology—Marxims, Leninism and Mao's thought—and to give them better awareness of the needs and aspirations of the people. The year's course is comprised of three parts: the study of Marx, Lenin and Mao, particpation in work on the farm lands of the school, and a month of work in a production brigade of a local commune. The latter two are intended to give the cadre a feeling for the lot of the peasants so they will serve the people more willingly when they return to their regular jobs. A saying in the school goes: "After you carry the shoulder pole (of the peasants), half your bureaucratic airs will be swept away." All cadre in the country, including high officials such as government ministers and ambassadors, are expected to attend a May Seventh school. Exceptions are only for those who are too old, who are not physically fit, who have unusual family requirements, or who cannot be spared from their jobs. Every government ministry has a May Seventh school as does the General Office of the Communist Party's Central Committee.

The reforms in education introduced at the time of the cultural revolution have repeatedly been termed "experimental," indicating that additional changes could come. The reforms have reflected more the ideological tendencies in the party than a pragmatic approach to learning. Whether current political trends will in time be translated into changes in the educational system remains to be seen. With increased emphasis on industrialization China may well have to place greater emphasis on technical and scientific training.

E. POPULATION

Chinese officials usually refer to their country's population as "800 million." The last census, in 1954, came up with a total of 582,603,417 for the mainland. Without evaluating how accurate that census may have been, the population of China has grown greatly since, and there is much uncertainty about the rate of increase. Officials readily admit that "800 million" is questionable. On my recent visit a high official said that the Ministry of Commerce used the figure 900 million but added that this total was probably exaggerated.

In his report to the Fourth National People's Congress in January 1975 Premier Chou En-lai said that China's population had increased sixty percent since liberation. The U.S. Department of Commerce has come up with two separate estimates of China's current population. The Bureau of the Census in a publication entitled *World Population: 1975*, estimates the mid-1975 population at 842,545,000. At a rate increase of about 12,000,000 a year which it posits, this would mean a population of 854,000,000 in mid-1976. But the Foreign Demographic

Analysis Division, in the same Department, estimates China's population, as of January 1, 1976, at 953,107,000. Lee Orleans, an authority in the Library of Congress on China's population, estimates the January 1, 1976, total at 863,000,000. Two other recently published estimates of China's population have been made by the Environmental Fund and by the Worldwatch Research Institute. The former places the mid-1976 population at 964.4 million and the latter estimates the current population at about 823 mililon—a difference of about 140 million.

Whatever the figure, the policy of the Chinese Government is to restrain the growth rate, except among the minorities. China encourages late marriages, at least age 28 for the men and 25 for women. The government promotes the use of birth control devices, contraceptives being supplied free through medical facilities throughout the nation. Education and social persuasion are used to induce couples to limit the number of children to no more than two. But one official acknowledged that birth control was difficult, especially in the countryside. Many people were still influenced, he said, by the Confucian idea that it is desirable to have many children. The government's goal is to reduce by 1980 the growth rate to 1.5 percent from the current level of some two percent. Progress is being made, however, as indicated by a .9 percent growth rate in theHua-hsi Brigade near Wuxi (Wushi). Hard, comprehensive statistics are a rarity, however, and only time will tell how effective the control program is in practice.

China's concern for population control is motivated, it is said, not by fear that population will outstrip food but in the interest of more rational planning, and of expanding the standard of living—more for everyone, better health, easing of burdens for parents, more work opportunities for women and superior education for children. Although the central government persists in applying the figure of "800 million" and has not itself publicly adopted the method of using local population estimates, observers in Hong Kong noted that the condolence messages published on the death of Chairman Mao state the number of people living in each province. These figures total 855 million.[21] However, one Chinese bureaucrat said that provincial population figures must also be taken with a grain of salt.

F. MEDICAL CARE

Medical care in China can be seen from two frames of reference. First, and most important, is the socio-political view. Here the measure is a comparison of health conditions in China before 1949 with those of today. By this standard the achievements are remarkable. Twenty-seven years ago no widespread system of medical care even existed. Malnutrition and starvation were everywhere, many diseases were rampant, and drug addiction and prostitution were common. Through basic public health measures, general improvements in the standard of living and the provision of medical care for all, these problems have been eliminated or, in the case of a few stubborn diseases, closely controlled. The other perspective is to look at how China's medical care system stands today qualitatively by Western standards. On the basis of that standard China's medical system

[21] See appendix F.

leaves much to be desired. But, as with any appraisal of how China's system is working, use of an external standard misses the political mark.

Barefoot doctors, now one and a half million strong, are the primary deliverers of health care in China. Generally, they are young men and women, selected by local community leaders, who receive about three months of training on the district level before returning to their commune or factory. The type and amount of training varies with local needs, but training in the use of acupuncture and Chinese herbal remedies, plus some Western antibiotics, are common to all programs. Several barefoot doctors have the responsibilities for the basic care of 800 to 1,500 people. A barefoot doctor functions in a semi-autonomous fashion. He is visited two or three times a year by medical doctors from the district hospital and can call on their help at any time. His duties include giving general physical examinations, emergency care, general immunization, distributing birth control devices, follow-up care for chronically-ill patients as determined by medical doctors, and general public health surveillance. His annual schedule generally consists of six months of work in providing health services, three months of work in the fields, and three months of continuing medical education at a medical facility. In actual practice the routine varies greatly depending on available relief, the type of facility, and the needs of the community. The key to progress in this system is continuing medical education. While improvements are being made, there is a difficult problem in this respect due to shortages of adequate facilities and trained personnel. Mobile medical teams of various specialities drawn from the district-level hospitals constantly tour facilities at lower levels on a rotational basis to upgrade local techniques and abilities. It was said that about one-fourth of the doctors in a large city hospital would be working in rural or remote areas at any given time.

Medical doctors now receive three years of formal training, but consideration is being given to shortening the program to two years. All medical schools teach both traditional Chinese medicine and Western medicine, with each school varying in its emphasis, depending on past orientation. The melding of the best of both systems has yet to be accomplished, but research efforts are being directed toward this goal. Specialty training has been shortened to emphasize the availability of care. For example, the national goal for neurosurgeons is one for every county in China. There are now two to three neurosurgeons per prefecture (10–12 counties in a prefecture) so the national goal appears attainable. This has been accomplished by reducing the time of training for neurosurgeons to three years of medical school, three years of general surgery and one year of neurosurgery. After this, the doctor is capable of performing "simple" neurosurgical procedures, judging his own capacity to handle more complicated operations. Should he desire to handle more difficult surgery, he generally learns through another surgeon, not through formal training. Like all government functionaries, medical personnel are urged to keep in tune with the needs and aspirations of the people and periodically spend six months to a year in a rural area, either doing manual labor or, in the case of doctors, aiding the local medical personnel.

At present venereal disease, leprosy, kala-azar, cholera, typhoid and polio are said to be non-existent. Tuberculosis and malaria are quite rare and malaria is localized to certain low-lying areas. Schistosomiasis (snail fever), a devastating disease in the past, has been closely controlled and no new cases have been reported recently. Alcoholism and drugs are not problems. Mental illness is quite rare, although there are some sanatoriums for treatment. Tremendous strides have been made in controlling disease through improvements in the standard of living, aggressive public health measures, stress on physical fitness, and an effective health care system.

Acupuncture both as a curative measure and as an anesthetic continues to enjoy a major position in Chinese medical care. As an anesthetic, it is said to be 90 percent successful. Its benefits include low cost, minimization of side effects, ease of administration and the patient's remaining conscious during surgery. As for the curative power of acupuncture, much scientific research is needed to come up with definitive findings. Claims of cures for diseases such as cholelithiasis, tic douloureux and deafness are but a few. Acupuncture kits are readily available to anyone for less than three dollars and acupuncture is frequently practiced by ordinary citizens. Research into both how and why acupuncture works and new usages is quite active at this time. Many questions remain unanswered, Chinese medical personnel admit.

There are three levels of medical institutions in the cities. First is the neighborhood or factory clinic which is responsible for routine care and emergency situations. It is usually staffed by several barefoot doctors. In the cities each large factory normally has its own hospital. For example, the July First Cotton Textile Mill Hospital we visited in Xinjiang (Sinkiang) province had 54 doctors manning a 200-bed hospital that served 8,300 workers and their families. While the laboratory and surgical facilities were somewhat rudimentary, a laser for opthamologic work had been in operation for a year, one of three in use in the province.

Next are hospitals at the district level. Here as many as several hundred health workers handle the more difficult cases, including complicated surgery. The education of physicians, barefoot doctors and other health personnel is handled in these facilities and some minor research is carried out. The provincial level hospital is larger and its staff is responsible for administrative and other matters for the province's medical system.

In the communes, each production team has health workers with somewhat less training that the barefoot doctor. The brigade level has a clinic staffed by several barefoot doctors, and at the commune level there is a small hospital, usually with a staff of about 40, including at least one fully-trained medical doctor, where minor surgery, limited hospitalization and continuing medical education are carried out. A network now exists throughout China where every citizen has ready access to some type of medical facility.

Medical care for factory workers and government functionaries is free and commune members pay only a nominal fee. Dependents of workers and functionaries may join a medical cooperative for 50 cents to $1 per year or pay 50 percent of their hospital bill. Daily care in a hospital for those few who must pay, costs approximately 60 cents per day, complicated brain or heart surgery runs $18–$20, and an appendectomy is $5. The average pay for doctors in a Shanghai hospital was $40 per month.

All medical research must be approved for funding by the central government. The thrust of the basic research effort is toward learning more about acupuncture and Chinese herbal medicine. Local research, however, is oriented toward more direct and short-term gains in health care. There have been notable medical advances in China. In burn therapy, for example, use of a salve made from a tree bark has enabled patients with 90 percent burns to survive and micro-surgical techniques for re-implantation of severed limbs, fingers, and toes by Chinese surgeons has generated great interest in the American medical community.

G. XINJIANG (SINKIANG): STRATEGIC BORDERLAND AND LAND OF MANY NATIONALITIES

The Xinjiang Uygur (Sinkiang Uighur) Autonomous Region, located in far northwest China, is the nation's largest province, comprising one-sixth of the total land area. Because of its size, resources and location, Xinjiang is of great geopolitical significance. Its frontier position in relation to the main population centers of China; its 3,100 miles of borders with the Soviet Union, India, Afghanistan, Pakistan and Mongolia; the Karamai oil field; the nuclear test site at Lop Nor; the presence of many non-Han nationalities, some of which spread across the border into the Soviet Union; the history of Soviet efforts to exert influence or control in this region in the past; and the richness of still undeveloped mineral resources all combine to make this an area worth special mention. I visited Xinjiang for a week.

The province is divided from East to West by the Tienshan mountain range. The Dzungarian basin to the north receives summer rainfall and is ideal for grazing land. There is also a great deal of irrigated farm land. I visited the capital, Urumqi (Urumchi), Shih Hotzu and the Turpan (Turfan) Depression in the central part of the Region. South of the Tienshan range, the Tarim Basin contains Takla Makan, one of the driest deserts in the world. Normal farming is carried on in small oases along the mountain escarpment in the south and around the other margins of the basin. In the southwest are the Pamir mountains called the "Roof of the World." The vast expanses of mountain and desert in the Region are inhospitable to settlement by large numbers of people. Nevertheless, about eleven million now inhabit the region and the total is rising due both to indigenous population growth and an influx of Han from other parts of China.

There have been incidents along the border with the Soviet Union from time to time and Soviet agents penetrate occasionally, but at present the border is relatively calm. However, military preparations are constant in the region and officials are confident of their ability to deal with any threat.

Traditionally Xinjiang's economy has been based on agriculture and herding. The Region's livestock includes one-fourth of China's sheep, yielding more than 60% of the nation's wool. State farms, whose paid employees are often Han Chinese from outside, occupy about 35 percent of the cultivated land and produce more than a quarter of the grain. Five hundred state farms, engaging in agriculture, animal husbandry and afforestation, have been set up by the central government. Grain and cotton are important crops. Others include potatoes and the famed fruit of Xinjiang, melons, grapes, peaches and apricots. Grain production, I was informed, has tripled over that of 1949, cotton has multiplied nine times since then, and livestock has more than doubled. Irrigation is vital to agriculture and numerous wells have been sunk and ingenious canals built to carry snow runoff from the mountains. Much of the massive winter-spring drives to improve farmland consist of clearing stony areas, converting desert areas into cropland, and expanding irrigation works. Before 1949 there was such little industry, local officials said, that even matches and nails had to be brought in from the outside. Now hundreds of factories and other installations produce iron, steel, coal, petroleum, electricity, nonferrous metals, machinery, leather, chemicals, textiles and food products. Available data show that in 1975 steel production was five times that of 1955, oil output double 1965, and fertilizer output eleven times that of 1965. Total industrial production in 1975 was termed an all time high. Output this year is said to be running ten percent above 1975.

The remoteness of Xinjiang from China's population centers and the scattered nature of its population make adequate transportation critical to development. Railways connect Xinjiang with Beijing (Peking) and 12,000 miles of highway link all parts of the region. Bus service goes to every county. Air service links Urumqi with towns in the region and with the national capital.

The central government, as a deliberate policy, helps develop the region's economy by preferential financing, by encouraging Han from eastern China to migrate there, and by various other means. Xinjiang is authorized to keep all local revenue for its own use and it also receives large subsidies from Beijing (Peking). Between 1955 and 1974 these subsidies amounted to 53% of the region's total revenue. The accelerated development policy for Xinjiang has a double aim: to strengthen the region as a national defense measure, and to integrate the local nationalities into Chinese life by allowing them to share the fruits of improving standards of living.

In my last report I described the general status of minorities in China, pointing out that non-Han peoples are concentrated in five Autonomous Regions, Nei Mongol (Inner Mongolia), Ningxia Huizu (Ningsia Hui), Xinjiang Uygur (Sinkiang Uighur), Xizang Izhiq (Tibet), and Guangxi Zhuangzu (Kwangsi Chuang). China asserts that it grants equality to all nationalities while simultaneously opposing Han chauvinism and local nationalism. The constitution permits minority nationalities the right of autonomy and under national law an autonomous region can enact supplementary regulations in political, economic, cultural and educational fields in accord with the characteristics, interests and needs of its nationalities.

In Xinjiang the status of the nationalities has many characteristics similar to those described for the areas covered in my earlier report, but there are differences. Historically the races and cultures of Sinkiang have sprung from a blending of many different peoples but today in Xinjiang the following nationality groups are identified. (See also the accompanying map).

Ethnolinguistic Groups

SINKIANG

ALTAIC*

TURKIC
1. Uighur
2. Kazakh
3. Kirghiz

4. Salar
5. Uzbek

MONGOLIAN
6. Mongol
7. Tung hsiang

8. Tu(Mongor)
9. Daur

TUNGUSIC
10. Oronchon
11. Sibo

12. Evenki

SINO-TIBETAN
▨ HAN (CHINESE)
△ HUI (CHINESE MUSLIM)

INDO-EUROPEAN
13. TADZHIK

*Language family

The Uygurs (Uighurs), a Turkic-speaking group, populating the central and southern portions of Xinjiang, have for many years been numerically dominant. The Kazakhs are relatively numerous in the northern and western portion of the region, including areas adjacent to the Soviet and Mongolian borders. Other nationalities are interspersed in the central area and the northern and western borderlands. They include Hui (Chinese Moslem), Mongols, Khalkhas, Kirghiz, Zibo, Manchu, Tadzhik, Russian, Uzbek, Tartar and Tibetan nationality groups. The Han Chinese, who historically were heavily outnumbered by the other nationalities, have entered the Region in large numbers since 1949 and especially since 1960. The influx is continuing and has changed markedly the ethnic balance of the Region. Part of the influx is due to the program sponsored generally throughout China for "educated" youth "to go to the countryside, to the mountains and to the borderlands." In Urumqi the following official figures showed the distribution of population in the Region in 1975:

Percentage of region's total population

Nationality group:

Uygur (Uighur)	45. 7
Han	41. 4
Kazakh	6. 4
Hui	4. 1
Mongol	0. 9
Khalkhas	0. 5
Zibo	0. 2
Tadzhik	0. 2
Others	0. 3

This breakdown shows the Uygurs as still the most numerous group. But it would not be surprising, if the inflow of Hans continues at the rate of recent years, that they would soon become the majority group in the Region. However, there is no indication that Han ethnic dominance would have adverse political or economic effects on the other nationalities. On the contrary, it appears that all nationalities in Xinjiang have benefitted without discrimination from the progress achieved in the past quarter of a century. Before 1949, the culture of the nationalities was on the verge of extinction, with illiteracy immense, the level of living very low and conflict among the groups not uncommon. The nationalities seem now to live in harmony and to benefit equally from the Region's economic progress. Certainly my observations in Urumqi, Shih-ho-tzu, and Turpan, lead me to believe that the various nationalities do intermingle, live and work together peacefully and without discernible discrimination. Cultural differences are outwardly most evident in the dress of some non-Han nationalities, particularly the women. Their colorful garb contrasts sharply with the standard blue and green clothing worn by the Han. I was told that the nationalities intermarry and from my visual impression of racial mixtures, this would seem to be true. In the sensitive matter of birth control, the PRC does not direct its program at the minority nationalities; in fact, it encourages large families and permits marriage at an age earlier than that applicable to the Han.

Use of their own languages by the nationalities, as guaranteed in the national constitution, is implemented in Xinjiang for four national groups. The Han, Uygur, Kazakh, and Mongolian languages are in use in local schools, publications, and radio. To illustrate, signs in Urumqi were in both Uygur and Han and the regional daily newspaper is published in all four languages. In the Number Five Municipal Primary School in Urumqi, for example, there were separate classes for the Uygur and the Han students, with each group being taught the other's language as a second language. One of the results of this practice is that many of the minority nationals are bilingual and some are trilingual. At Turpan, however, the leaders who received me did not understand Han and we communicated by an interpretation of Uygur to Han to English and back again. At the university level I was told that Han prevails although some classes are conducted in other languages.

One reform that I have not been able to evaluate is the recent introduction of the Latinized alphabet for Uygur and Kazakh. A new alphabet is also being prepared for Mongolian. The Latinized alphabet is a substitute for older Arabic scripts and is one part of a general movement for language reform throughout China. Since Latinization is based on the new Chinese phonetic system, the result has been characterized as two new languages capable of being understood and easily learned by both the nationalities and the Han. Another result would be the creation of a written linguistic barrier between members of the same nationality groups now separated by the closed Soviet-Chinese border. The new alphabet is in use, but only about half the school children have learned it and many adults have not yet received instruction.

The governing body of Xinjiang is authorized to organize local public security forces, manage local finance, and enact legal regulations but it is still subject to central government control in administration, planning, military, educational and propaganda matters as are other Chinese provinces. The local government may draw up statutes and regulations, but they can be vetoed by the Standing Committee of the National People's Congress (NPC) in Beijing (Peking). The national minorities of Xinjiang, however, are represented in the NPC. It was reported in 1975 that 67 percent of Xinjiang's deputies to the NPC were from minorities. The Standing Committee of the People's Congress has three members from Sinkiang's minorities. Minorities were also represented substantially among the members of the regional, county and municipal governing bodies whom I met in Xinjiang. In fact, Chinese sources say that minority nationalities occupy the majority of seats in Xinjiang's People's Congress and revolutionary committees at all levels. An indication of the political status of the nationalities is their participation in the Party. Saifudin, a Uygur, is First Secretary of the Region's Communist Party, an Alternate Member of the Politburo of the Chinese Communist Party, Chairman of the Region's Revolutionary Committee, and the Political Commissar of the Xinjiang Military Region. Although absolute figures were not available to me, I was told that the number of minorities in the regional party has increased sixteen times since 1955. Clearly, the authorities desire to demonstrate that the minorities enjoy a substantial slice of political power.

V. CONCLUDING COMMENTS

China is a vast land of talented and industrious people, with a rich recorded history going back more than three thousand years. It is old. We are young. There is much that we can learn from one another. The beginning of wisdom is to understand how little we know. The track record of the China "experts" in the post-1949 period leaves much to be desired. Moreover, concentration on China's leadership struggles has, unfortunately, distracted attention from the all-important fact that the immense power of China's people and resources has been harnessed as never before in history.

We are vastly different countries in our culture, language, political ideology, and in the way we view ourselves and the outside world. We have a tendency to fluctuate to extreme attitudes towards the Chinese as with other people abroad. Having reestablished friendly contact we need not go overboard on China. The Chinese have no need for it; nor do we.

Nor should Chinese society be judged by American standards. It is a disciplined society with its people subjected to unremitting propaganda from an all-pervasive party-government apparatus. Westerners note the absence of individual freedoms in China and the subservience to an all-powerful state. On the other hand, the Chinese see our society as wasteful and disorganized. In fact, present conditions in the two nations are so different that to compare the two is to compare apples and oranges.

To weigh the United States-China relationship in a reasonable context, Americans must look at common interests, not at our differences. That is what has brought the two countries together, almost in spite of themselves, in an official but unorthodox relationship.

We are both greatly concerned about the Soviet Union and its intentions.

We both have a need for better mutual understanding to avoid future miscalculations.

We have a common interest in the moderation of tensions in Asia and in seeing that the nations in the area remain free of domination by outside powers.

We both desire a viable Japan free of the danger of militarism.

We both seek a better world for the future generations in our respective countries.

The initial stage of China's revolution against warlordism, corruption, and outside domination was concluded twenty-seven years ago. "When people are poor, they will work harder for change; when people are oppressed they will strive for revolution. Two hundred years ago your people also understood such experiences," a leader in Shanghai said to me.

For more than two decades the United States closed its official mind to China and the channels of effective communication between the two nations were blocked. The consequences of this period of know-nothingness still linger. Miscalculations about China may well have been the main factor in the involvement of the United States in two major wars in Asia in a single generation. Pressures are at work which could cause another major miscalculation over Taiwan.

The national interest is deeply involved, in my judgment, in moving without further delay to settle the Taiwan problem. Gambling for more time? For what? Further delay could well prove to be another in the long series of disastrous miscalculations which have afflicted U.S. foreign policy in Asia since World War II. Solving this problem will put the United States in a unique position in the triangular relationship. If we act more wisely than in the past, we will act now, not on the basis of emotional catch-phrases, but on the basis of rational contemporary American interests in the Western Pacific. Fundamental to the safeguarding of these interests, is an open diplomatic door between the government of what will soon be a billion Chinese, organized in a dynamic technological state, and the government of the people of the United States.

APPENDIXES

APPENDIX A

CHRONOLOGY OF THE VISIT TO THE PEOPLE'S REPUBLIC OF CHINA,
SEPTEMBER 21–OCTOBER 12, 1976

Tuesday, September 21, 1976

Morning: Arrived Shanghai by air from Guam. Received by representatives of the Chinese People's Institute of Foreign Affairs who outlined itinerary and accompanied the mission throughout the visit.

Afternoon: Travelled by train to Wuxi (Wu-hsi). Given boat tour of Lake Tai-hu.

Wednesday, September 22, 1976

All day: Visited Hua-hsi Brigade, a model farm near Wuxi (Wu-hsi).

Thursday, September 23, 1976

Morning: Left Wuxi (Wu-hsi) by train. Arrived Nanjing (Nanking).

Afternoon: Toured Yangtze River aboard a People's Liberation Army boat. Visited and was briefed on Yangtze River Bridge. Visited mausoleum of Dr. Sun Yet-Sen.

Friday, September 24, 1976

Morning: Visited Nanjing (Nanking) Teachers College. Observed various class demonstrations and performances by students.

Afternoon: Left Nanjing (Nanking) by commercial airline (CAAC). Arrived Beijing (Peking).

Evening: Briefed at U.S. Liaison Office by Ambassador Thomas Gates and staff.

Saturday, September 25, 1976

Morning: Left Beijing (Peking) by CAAC. Arrived Urumqi (Urumchi), capital of Xinjiang Uygur (Sinkiang Uighur) Autonomous Region. Received and briefed by representatives of Revolutionary Committee of region.

Afternoon: Visited the Exhibition of the Twentieth Anniversary of the Founding of Xinjiang Uygur (Sinkiang Uighur) Autonomous Region.

Sunday, September 26, 1976

Morning: Left Urumqi (Urumchi) by auto. Arrived Shih Ho-tzu.

Afternoon. Visited August First Woolen Mill and August First Sugar Refinery.

Monday, September 27, 1976

Morning: Visited Number 143 State Farm.

Afternoon: Conversation with "educated youth." Departed Shih Ho-tzu by auto.

Evening: Arrived Urumqui (Urumchi).

Tuesday, September 28, 1976

Morning: Visited July First Cotton Textile Mill.

Afternoon: Visited the Exhibition of Historic and Archaelogical Finds of Xinjiang Uygur (Sinkiang Uighur) Antonomous Region.

Evening: Toured department store in Urumqi (Urumchi).

Wednesday, September 29, 1976

Morning: Departed Urumqi (Urumchi) by auto.

Afternoon: Arrived Turpan (Turfan). Briefed by the Vice Chairman of the Revoluntionary Committee of Turpan (Turfan) County. Visited Five Star Commune.

Thursday, September 30, 1976

Morning: Visited the ancient ruins of Kaochang City. Visited the Wine and Fruit Factory of Turpan (Turfan).

Afternoon: Visited the Grape Commune in Grape Vine Valley. Left Turpan (Turfan) by auto.

Evening: Arrived Urumqi (Urumchi).

Friday, October 1, 1976

All day: Visited Tien Chih (Heavenly Lake) in the Tienshan Mountains.

Evening: Dinner with officials of the regional Revolutionary Committee in Urumqi (Urumchi).

Saturday, October 2, 1976

Morning: Visited Number 5 Municipal Primary School.

Afternoon: Left Urumqi (Urumchi) by commercial air (CAAC). Arrived Beijing (Peking).

Sunday, October 3, 1976

Morning: Left Beijing (Peking) by commercial air (CAAC).

Afternoon: Arrived Guangzhou (Canton)) after stop over at Hangzhou (Hang-chou). Left for Taishan by auto.

Evening: Arrived at Taishan in Guangdong (Kwangtung) province.

Monday, October 4, 1976

Morning: Visited the Yunghe Production Team, Nanyang Production Brigade, Tuanfen Peoples Commune, in an area from which in the past many Chinese have emigrated to the United States.

Afternoon: Visited the Number One Farm Machinery Factory and the Taishan Porcelain Factory.

Evening: Attended volley ball games played by Taishan championship women's and men's teams.

Tuesday, October 5, 1976

Morning: Left Taishan by auto for Hsinhui. Enroute inspected the hydro-electric project in the Kutou Mountains.

Afternoon: Arrived Hsinhui. Visited the Hsinhui Farm Machinery Factory and the Artistic Palm Products Factory.

Evening: Attended training demonstration by young people's swimming school.

Wednesday, October 6, 1976

Morning: Left Hsinhui by auto.
Afternoon: Arrived Guangzhou (Canton). Left Guangzhou (Canton) by air for Beijing (Peking).
Evening: Arrived Beijing (Peking).

Thursday, October 7, 1976

Morning: Met with Ambassador Youde, British Ambassador to the People's Republic of China.
Afternoon: Met with Vice Foreign Minister Wang Hai-jung.
Evening: Informal dinner with Madam Vice Foreign Minister and Dr. Chou Pei-yuan, Vice Director, Chinese People's Institute of Foreign Affairs.

Friday, October 8, 1976

Morning: Visited the Great Wall and Ming Tombs.
Afternoon: Met with Dr. George Hatem.
Evening: Attended dinner hosted by Mr. David Dean, acting head of the U.S. Liaison Office in the absence of Ambassador Gates.

Saturday, October 9, 1976

Morning: Visited May Seventh Cadre School for Eastern District of Beijing (Peking).
Afternoon: Met with Vice-Premier Li Hsien-nien in the Great Hall of the People.

Sunday, October 10, 1976

Morning: Traveled from Beijing (Peking) to Shanghai by commercial air (CAAC).
Afternoon: Visited Tienshan Workers New Residential Area.
Evening: Attended dinner hosted by Feng Kuo-chu, Vice Chairman of Municipal Revolutionary Committee of Shanghai.

Monday, October 11, 1976

Morning: Visited and observed acupuncture anasthesia surgery performed in Huashan Hospital of Shanghai. Some members of mission visited Shanghai Turbo-generator Factory in Minhang.
Evening: Hosted dinner for escorts from Chinese People's Institute of Foreign Affairs.

Tuesday, October 12, 1976

Morning: After inspection of central city of Shanghai departed China by air.

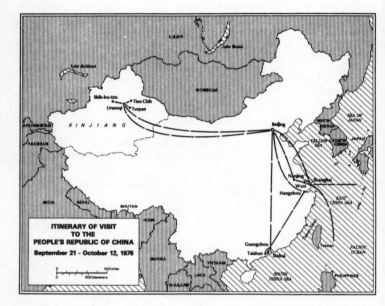

ITINERARY OF VISIT
TO THE
PEOPLE'S REPUBLIC OF CHINA
September 21 - October 12, 1976

APPENDIX B

MUTUAL DEFENSE TREATY BETWEEN THE UNITED STATES OF AMERICA AND THE REPUBLIC OF CHINA

Signed at Washington December 2, 1954; Ratification advised by the Senate of the United States of American February 9, 1955; Ratified by the President of the United States of America February 11, 1955; Ratified by the Republic of China February 15, 1955; Ratifications exchanged at Taipei March 3, 1955; Proclaimed by the President of the United States of America April 1, 1955; Entered into force March 3, 1955

The Parties to this Treaty,

Reaffirming their faith in the purposes and principles of the Charter of the United Nations and their desire to live in peace with all peoples and all Governments, and desiring to strengthen the fabric of peace in the West Pacific Area,

Recalling with mutual pride the relationship which brought their two peoples together in a common bond of sympathy and mutual ideals to fight side by side against imperialist aggression during the last war,

Desiring to declare publicly and formally their sense of unity and their common determinations to defend themselves against external armed attack, so that no potential aggressor could be under the illusion that either of them stands alone in the West Pacific Area, and

Desiring further to strengthen their present efforts for collective defense for the preservation of peace and security pending the development of a more comprehensive system of regional security in the West Pacific Area,

Have agreed as follows:

ARTICLE I

The Parties undertake, as set forth in the Charter of the United Nations, to settle any international dispute in which they may be involved by peaceful means in such a manner that international peace, security and justice are not endangered and to refrain in their international relations from the threat or use of force in any manner inconsistent with the purposes of the United Nations.

ARTICLE II

In order more effectively to achieve the objective of this Treaty, the Parties separately and jointly by self-help and mutual aid will maintain and develop their individual and collective capacity to resist armed attack and communist subversive activities directed from without against their territorial integrity and political stability.

ARTICLE III

The Parties undertake to strengthen their free institutions and to cooperate with each other in the development of economic progress and social well-being and to further their individual and collective efforts towards these ends.

ARTICLE IV

The Parties, through their Foreign Ministers or their deputies, will consult together from time to time regarding the implementation of this Treaty.

ARTICLE V

Each Party recognizes than an armed attack in the West Pacific Area directed against the territories of either of the Parties would be dangerous to its own peace and safety and declares that it would act to meet the common danger in accordance with its constitutional processes.

Any such armed attack and all measures taken as a result thereof shall be immediately reported to the Security Council of the United Nations. Such measures shall be terminated when the Security Council has taken the measures necessary to restore and maintain international peace and security.

ARTICLE VI

For the purposes of Articles II and V, the terms "territorial" and "territories" shall mean in respect of the Republic of China, Taiwan and the Pescadores; and in respect of the United States of America, the island territories in the West Pacific under its jurisdiction. The provisions of Articles II and V will be applicable to such other territories as may be determined by mutual agreement.

ARTICLE VII

The Government of the Republic of China grants, and the Government of the United States of America accepts, the right to dispose such United States land, air and sea forces in and about Taiwan and the Pescadores as may be required for their defense, as determined by mutual agreement.

ARTICLE VIII

This Treaty does not affect and shall not be interpreted as affecting in any way the rights and obligations of the Parties under the Charter of the United Nations or the responsibility of the United Nations for the maintenance of international peace and security.

ARTICLE IX

This Treaty shall be ratified by the United States of America and the Republic of China in accordance with their respective constitutional processes and will come into force when instruments of ratification thereof have been exchanged by them at Taipei.

ARTICLE X

This Treaty shall remain in force indefinitely. Either Party may terminate it one year after notice has been given to the other Party.

Statements by and Exchange of Notes Between Secretary of State John Foster Dulles and Foreign Minister George K. C. Yeh Upon the Occasion of the Signing of the Mutual Defense Treaty Between the United States of America and the Republic of China at Washington

STATEMENTS MADE DECEMBER 2, 1954

Secretary Dulles:

It is a great pleasure to welcome Foreign Minister Yeh, Ambassador Koo, and the members of his staff here this afternoon for the signing of this Mutual Defense Treaty between the United States and the Republic of China. I wholly concur in what President Chiang Kai-shek said in his message to me yesterday, that " a necessary link in the chain of Far Eastern defense has now been forged." It is my hope that the signing of this Defense Treaty will put to rest once and for all rumors and reports that the United States will in any manner agree to the abandonment of Formosa and the Pescadores to Communist control. The signing of this treaty is not only an expression of the good will and friendship existing between the Governments of the United States and of Free China, but also of the abiding friendship of the people of the United States for the Chinese people.

Foreign Minister Yeh:

It has been my privilege and honor to be associated with Mr. Dulles in the making and signing of this Treaty of Mutual Defense between my country and the United States of America. I am happy to recall that throughout the negotiations for this treaty, conducted at Taipei and Washington, we have been guided by the principle of mutuality and the spirit of friendly cooperation.

It is the hope of my Government that this treaty will serve to promote the common cause of freedom, particularly at this juncture of the world situation.

EXCHANGE OF NOTES

DEPARTMENT OF STATE,
Washington, December 10, 1954.

His Excellency GEORGE K. C. YEH,
Minister of Foreign Affairs of the Republic of China.

EXCELLENCY: I have the honor to refer to recent conversations between representatives of our two Governments and to confirm the understandings reached as a result of those conversations, as follows:

The Republic of China effectively controls both the territory described in Article VI of the Treaty of Mutual Defenses between the Republic of China and the United States of America signed on December 2, 1954, at Washington and other territory. It possesses with respect to all territory now and hereafter under its control the inherent right of self-defense. In view of the obligations of the two Parties under the said Treaty, and of the fact that the use of force from either of these areas by either of the Parties affects the other, it is agreed that such use of force will be a matter of joint agreement, subject to action of an emergency character which is clearly an exercise of the inherent right of self-defense. Military elements which are a product of joint effort and contribution by the two Parties will not be removed from the territories described in Article VI to a degree which would substantially diminish the defensibility of such territories without mutual agreement.

Accept, Excellency, the assurances of my highest consideration.

/s/ JOHN FOSTER DULLES,
Secretary of State of the United States of America.

———

DECEMBER 10, 1954.

His Excellency JOHN FOSTER DULLES,
Secretary of State of the United States of America.

EXCELLENCY : I have the honor to acknowledge the receipt or Your Excellency's Note of today's date, which reads as follows :

"I have the honor to refer to recent conversations between representatives of our two Governments and to confirm the understandings reached as a result of those conversations, as follows :

"The Republic of China effectively controls both the territory described in Article VI of the Treaty of Mutual Defense between the Republic of China and the United States of America signed on December 2, 1954, at Washington and other territory. It possesses with respect to all territory now and hereafter under its control the inherent right of self-defense. In view of the obligations of the two Parties under the said Treaty and of the fact that the use of force from either of these areas by either of the Parties affects the other, it is agreed that such use of force will be a matter of joint agreement, subject to action of an emergency character which is clearly an exercise of the inherent right of self-defense. Military elements which are a product of joint effort and contribution by the two Parties will not be removed from the territories described in Article VI to a degree which would substantially diminish the defensibility of such territories without mutual agreement."

I have the honor to confirm, on behalf of my Government, the understanding set forth in Your Excellency's Note under reply.

I avail myself of this opportunity to convey to Your Excellency the assurances of my highest consideration.

GEORGE K. C. YEH,
Minister for Foreign Affairs of the Republic of China.

APPENDIX C

TEXT OF PROPOSALS DURING 1955–56 NEGOTIATIONS CONCERNING THE RENUNCIATION OF FORCE

1. United States Statement and Proposal on Renunciation of Force, October 8, 1955

One of the practical matters for discussion between us is that each of us should renounce the use of force to achieve our policies when they conflict. The United States and the PRC [People's Republic of China] confront each other with policies which are in certain respects incompatible. This fact need not, however, mean armed conflict, and the most important single thing we can do is first of all to be sure that it will not lead to armed conflict.

Then and only then can other matters causing tension between the parties in the Taiwan area and the Far East be hopefully discussed.

It is not suggested that either of us should renounce any policy objectives which we consider we are legitimately entitled to achieve, but only that we renounce the use of force to implement these policies.

Neither of us wants to negotiate under the threat of force. The free discussion of differences, and their fair and equitable solution, become impossible under the overhanging threat that force may be resorted to when one party does not agree with the other.

The United States as a member of the United Nations has agreed to refrain in its international relations from the threat or use of force. This has been its policy for many years and is its guiding principle of conduct in the Far East, as throughout the world.

The use of force to achieve national objectives does not accord with accepted standards of conduct under international law.

The Covenant of the League of Nations, the Kellogg-Briand Treaties, and the Charter of the United Nations reflect the universal view of the civilized community of nations that the use of force as an instrument of national policy violates international law, constitutes a threat to international peace, and prejudices the interests of the entire world community.

There are in the world today many situations which tempt those who have force to use it to achieve what they believe to be legitimate policy objectives. Many countries are abnormally divided or contain what some consider to be abnormal intrusions. Nevertheless, the responsible governments of the world have in each of these cases renounced the use of force to achieve what they believe to be legitimate and even urgent goals.

It is an essential foundation and preliminary to the success of the discussions under Item 2 that it first be made clear that the parties to these discussions renounce the use of force to make the policies of either prevail over those of the other. That particularly applies to the Taiwan area.

The acceptance of this principle does not involve third parties, or the justice or injustice of conflicting claims. It only involves recognizing and agreeing to abide by accepted standards of international conduct.

We ask, therefore, as a first matter for discussion under Item 2, a declaration that your side will not resort to the use of force in the Taiwan area except defensively. The United States would be prepared to make a corresponding declaration. These declarations will make it appropriate for us to pass on to the discussion of other matters with a better hope of coming to constructive conclusions.

2. Chinese Draft Declaration on Renunciation of Force, October 27, 1955

1. Ambassador Wang Ping-nan on behalf of the Government of the People's Republic of China and Ambassador U. Alexis Johnson on behalf of the Government of the United States of America jointly declare that,

2. In accordance with Article 2, Paragraph 3, of the Charter of the United Nations, "All members shall settle their international disputes by peaceful means in such a manner that international peace and security, and justice, are not endangered"; and

3. In accordance with Article 2, Paragraph 4 of the Charter of the United Nations, "All members shall refrain in their international relations from the threat or use of force against the territorial integrity or political independence of any state, or in any other manner inconsistent with the purposes of the United Nations";

4. The People's Republic of China and the United States of America agree that they should settle disputes between their two countries by peaceful means without resorting to the threat or use of force.

5. In order to realize their common desire, the People's Republic of China and the United States of America decide to hold a conference of Foreign Ministers to settle through negotiations the question of relaxing and eliminating the tension in Taiwan area.

3. United States Draft Declaration on Renunciation of Force, November 10, 1955

1. The Ambassador of the United States of America and the Ambassador of the People's Republic of China during the course of the discussions of practical matters at issue have expressed the determination that the differences between the two sides shall not lead to armed conflict.

2. They recognize that the use of force to achieve national objectives does not accord with the principles and purposes of the United Nations Charter or with generally accepted standards of international conduct.

3. They furthermore recognize that the renunciation of the threat or use of force is essential to the just settlement of disputes or situations which might lead to a breach of the peace.

Therefore, without prejudice to the pursuit by each side of its policies by peaceful means they have agreed to announce the following declarations:

5. Ambassador Wang Ping-nan informed Ambassador U. Alexis Johnson that:

6. In general, and with particular reference to the Taiwan area, the People's Republic of China renounces the use of force, except in individual and collective self-defense.

7. Ambassador U. Alexis Johnson informed Ambassador Wang Ping-nan that:

8. In general, and with particular reference to the Taiwan area, the United States renounces the use of force, except in individual and collective self-defense.

4. Chinese Draft Counterproposal for an Agreed Announcement, December 1, 1955

1. Ambassador Wang Ping-nan, on behalf of the Government of the People's Republic of China, and Ambassador Alexis Johnson, on behalf of the Government of the United States of America, agree to announce:

2. The People's Republic of China and the United States of America are determined that they should settle disputes between their two countries through peaceful negotiations without resorting to the threat or use of force;

3. The two Ambassadors should continue their talks to seek practical and feasible means for the realization of this common desire.

5. United States Revision of Chinese December 1 Counterproposal, January 12, 1956

1. Ambassador Wang Ping-nan, on behalf of the Government of the People's Republic of China, and Ambassador U. Alexis Johnson, on behalf of the Government of the United States of America, agree to announce:

2. The People's Republic of China and the United States of America are determined that they will settle disputes between them through peaceful means and that, without prejudice to the inherent right of individual and colelctive self-defense, they will not resort to the threat or use of force in the Taiwan area or elsewhere.

3. The two Ambassadors should continue their talks to seek practical and feasible means for the realization of this common desire.

6. United States Draft Proposal for Announcement of April 19, 1956

1. Ambassador U. Alexis Johnson, on behalf of the Government of the United States of America, and Ambassador Wang Ping-nan, on behalf of the Government of the People's Republic of China, agree, without prejudice to the pursuit by each side of its policies by peaceful means or its inherent right of individual or collective self-defense, to announce:

2. The United States of America and the People's Republic of China are determined that they should settle disputes between their two countries through peaceful negotiations without resorting to the threat or use of force in the Taiwan area or elsewhere.

3. The two Ambassadors should continue their talks to seek practical and feasible means for the realization of this common desire.

7. Chinese Draft Counterproposal for an Agreed Announcement, May 11, 1956

1. Ambassador Wang Pin-nan, on behalf of the Government of the People's Republic of China, and Ambassador U. Alexis Johnson, on behalf of the Government of the United States of America, agree, without prejudice to the principles of mutual respect for territorial integrity and sovereignty and non-interference in each other's internal affairs, to announce:

2. The People's Republic of China and the United States of America are determined that they should settle disputes between their two countries in the Taiwan area through peaceful negotiations without resorting to the threat or use of force against each other;

3. The two ambassadors should continue their talks to seek and to ascertain within two months practical and feasible means for the realization of this common desire, including the holding of a Sino-American conference of the foreign ministers, and to make specific arrangements.

Sources : 1–5. Department of State Bulletin, Jan. 30, 1956, pp. 166–167.
6. Department of State Bulletin, June 25, 1956, p. 1070.
7. New China News Agency Bulletin No. 1579, June 13, 1956, pp. 7–8.

APPENDIX D

DIPLOMATIC RELATIONS OF THE REPUBLIC OF CHINA AND THE PEOPLE'S REPUBLIC OF CHINA

As of August 30, 1976, 26 countries have diplomatic relations with the Republic of China and 110 have established or have announced establishment of diplomatic relations with the People's Republic of China. A list of the countries which recognize and/or have official relations with the two governments follows:

1. REPUBLIC OF CHINA

A. COUNTRIES HAVING DIPLOMATIC RELATIONS WITH THE REPUBLIC OF CHINA (ROC) (26)

Barbados	Lesotho
Bolivia	Liberia
Colombia	Libya [1]
Costa Rica	Malawi
Dominican Republic	Nicaragua
El Salvador	Panama
Guatemala	Paraguay
Haiti	Saudi Arabia
Holy See	South Africa (April 1976)
Honduras	Swaziland
Ivory Coast	Tonga (April 1972)
Jordan	United States
Republic of Korea	Uruguay

B. COUNTRIES HAVING CONSULAR RELATIONS ONLY WITH THE REPUBLIC OF CHINA (1)

Nauru (August 1975)

2. PEOPLE'S REPUBLIC OF CHINA

A. COUNTRIES HAVING DIPLOMATIC RELATIONS WITH THE PEOPLE'S REPUBLIC OF CHINA (PRC) (110), WITH DATE OF THE ESTABLISHMENT OF RELATIONS

Afghanistan (Jan. 1955)	Bangladesh (Oct. 1975)
Albania (Nov. 1949)	Belgium (Oct. 1971)
Algeria (Sept. 1958 with Provisional Govt.)	Botswana (Jan. 1975)
Argentina (Feb. 1972)	Brazil (Aug. 1974)
Australia (Dec. 1972)	Bulgaria (Oct. 1949)
Austria (May 1971)	Burma (June 1950)
	Burundi (resumed Oct. 1971)

---

[1] Libya has unilaterally announced recognition of the PRC but retains relations with the ROC.

147

Cambodia (July 1958)
Cameroon (March 1971)
Canada (Oct. 1970)
Cape Verde Islands (April 1976)
Central African Republic (Resumed Aug. 1976)
Chad (Nov. 1972)
Chile (Dec. 1970)
Comoro Islands (Nov. 1975)
Congo (Brazzaville) (Feb. 1964)
Cuba (Sept. 1960)
Cyprus (Jan. 1972)
Czechoslovakia (Oct. 1949)
Dahomey (resumed Dec. 1972)
Denmark (May 1950)
Egypt (May 1956)
Equatorial Guinea (Oct. 1970)
Ethiopia (Dec. 1970)
Federal Republic of Germany (Oct. 1950)
Fiji Islands (Nov. 1975)
Finland (Oct. 1950)
France (Jan. 1964)
Gabon (March 1974)
Gambia (Dec. 1974)
German Democratic Republic (Oct. 1949)
Ghana (resumed Feb. 1972)
Greece (June 1972)
Guinea (Oct. 1959)
Guinea-Bissau (Sept. 1974)
Guyana (June 1972)
Hungary (Oct. 1949)
Iceland (Dec. 1971)
India (April 1950)
Iran (Aug. 1971)
Iraq (Aug. 1958)
Italy (Nov. 1970)
Jamaica (Nov. 1972)
Japan (Sept. 1972)
Kenya (Dec. 1963)
Kuwait (March 1971)
Laos (Sept. 1962)
Lebanon (Nov. 1971)
Luxembourg (Nov. 1972)
Malagasy Republic (Nov. 1972)
Malaysia (May 1974)
Maldives (Oct. 1972)
Mali (Oct. 1960)
Malta (Jan. 1972)
Mauritania (July 1965)
Mauritius (April 1972)

Mexico (Feb. 1972)
Mongolia (Oct. 1949)
Morocco (Nov. 1958)
Mozambique (June 1975)
Nepal (Aug. 1955)
Netherlands (Nov. 1954)
New Zealand (Dec. 1972)
Niger (July 1974)
Nigeria (Feb. 1971)
North Korea (Oct. 1949)
Norway (Oct. 1954)
Pakistan (May 1951)
Papua New Guinea (Oct. 1976)
People's Democratic Republic of Yemen (Feb. 1968)
Peru (Nov. 1971)
Philippines (June 1975)
Poland (Oct. 1949)
Romania (Oct. 1949)
Rwanda (Nov. 1971)
Sao Tome and Principe (July 1975)
Senegal (Dec. 1971)
Seychelles Islands (June 1976)
Sierra Leone (July 1971)
Somalia (Dec. 1960)
Spain (March 1973)
Sri Lanka (Feb. 1957)
Sudan (Dec. 1958)
Surinam (May 1976)
Sweden (May 1959)
Switzerland (Sept. 1950)
Syria (Aug. 1956)
Tanzania (Oct. 1964)
Thailand (July 1975)
Togo (Sept. 1972)
Trinidad and Tobago (June 1974)
Tunisia (resumed Oct. 1971)
Turkey (Aug. 1971)
Uganda (Oct. 1962)
United Kingdom (June 1954)
Upper Volta (Sept. 1973)
USSR (Oct. 1949)
Venezuela (June 1974)
Vietnam (Jan. 1950)[2]
Western Samoa (Nov. 1975)
Yemen Arab Republic (Aug. 1956)
Yugoslavia (Jan. 1955)
Zaire (Nov. 1972)
Zambia (Oct. 1964)

---

[2] Prior to the formation of the Socialist Republic of Vietnam (July 1976) PRC had separate relations with North Vietnam (Jan. 1950) and the Provisional Revolutionary Government of South Vietnam (June 1969).

B. COUNTRIES HAVING CONSULAR RELATIONS ONLY WITH THE PEOPLE'S
REPUBLIC OF CHINA (1), WITH DATE OF ESTABLISHMENT OF RELATIONS

San Marino (May 1971)

C. COUNTRIES WHICH RECOGNIZE, BUT HAVE NO RELATIONS WITH, THE
PEOPLE'S REPUBLIC OF CHINA (5), WITH DATE OF RECOGNITION

Bhutan (Oct. 1971)[3]   Israel (Jan. 1950)[4]
Portugal (Jan. 1975)   Libya (June 1971) (See
Indonesia (April 1950)   footnote 1, p. 1)

D. COUNTRIES WHICH THE PRC HAS UNILATERALLY RECOGNIZED, BUT HAVE
NO RELATIONS WITH THE PRC (2)

Brahamas (July 1973)
Grenada (Feb. 1974)

3. COUNTRIES WHICH NEITHER RECOGNIZE NOR HAVE RELATIONS WITH
THE REPUBLIC OF CHINA OR THE PEOPLE'S REPUBLIC OF CHINA (10)

Angola   Ireland
Bahamas   Oman
Bahrain   Qatar
Ecuador[5]   Singapore[6]
Grenada   United Arab Emirates

[3] Recognition based on vote in UN to admit PRC and expel ROC.
[4] Israel has not been recognized by the PRC.
[5] Ecuador has broken relations with the ROC but has not formally recognized the PRC.
[6] Singapore has permitted the ROC to establish a trade mission which also handles consular matters. Singapore does not consider this as recognition and has no mission on Taiwan.

Source : Department of State.

APPENDIX E

SPEECH BY PREMIER CHOU EN-LAI

REPORT ON THE WORK OF THE GOVERNMENT

(Delivered on January 13, 1975 at the First Session of the Fourth
National People's Congress of the People's Republic of China)

Fellow Deputies!

In accordance with the decision of the Central Committee of the
Communist Party of China, I shall make a report on behalf of the
State Council to the Fourth National People's Congress on the work
of the government.

Since the Third National People's Congress, the most important
event in the political life of the people of all nationalities in our country has been the Great Proletarian Cultural Revolution personally initiated and led by our great leader Chairman Mao. In essence this is a
great political revolution carried out by the proletariat against the
bourgeoisie and all other exploiting classes. It destroyed the bourgeois
headquarters of Liu Shaochi and of Lin Piao and smashed their plots
to restore capitalism. The current nation-wide movement to criticize
Lin Piao and Confucius is the continuation and deepening of this great
revolution. The victory of the Great Proletarian Cultural Revolution
has consolidated the dictatorship of the proletariat in our country,
promoted socialist construction and ensured that our country would
stand on the side of the oppressed people and oppressed nations of the
world. The cultural revolution has provided new experience on continuing the revolution under the dictatorship of the proletariat; its
historical significance is great and its influence far-reaching.

In the course of the Great Proletarian Cultural Revolution and the
movement to criticize Lin Piao and Confucius, our people of all nationalities have unfolded a mass movement to study Marxism-Leninism-Mao Tsetung Thought and thus heightened their awareness of
class struggle and the struggle between the two lines, and struggle-
criticism-transformation in the superstructure has achieved major successes. The three-in-one revolutionary committees composed of the old,
the middle-aged and the young have forged closer links with the
masses. Successors to the cause of the proletarian revolution are ma-
turing in large numbers. The proletarian revolution in literature and
art exemplified by the model revolutionary theatrical works is developing in depth. The revolution in education and in health work is thriv-
ing. The cadres and the workers, peasants, soldiers, students and commercial workers are perservering on the May 7th road. Over a million
barefoot doctors are becoming more competent. Nearly ten million
school graduates have gone to mountainous and other rural areas. With

the participation of workers, peasants and soldiers the Marxist theoretical contingents are expanding. The emergence of all these new things has strengthened the all-round dictatorship of the proletariat over the bourgeoisie in the realm of the superstructure, and this further helps consolidate and develop the socialist economic base.

We have overfulfilled the Third Five-Year Plan and will successfully fulfill the Fourth Five-Year Plan in 1975. Our country has won good harvests for thirteen years running. The total value of agricultural output for 1974 is estimated to be 51 per cent higher than that for 1964. This fully demonstrates the superiority of the people's commune. While China's population has increased 60 per cent since the liberation of the country, grain output has increased 140 per cent and cotton 470 per cent. In a country like ours with a population of nearly 800 million, we have succeeded in ensuring the people their basic needs in food and clothing. Gross industrial output for 1974 is estimated to be 190 per cent more than 1964, and the output of major products has greatly increased. Steel has increased 120 per cent, coal 91 per cent, petroleum 650 per cent, electric power, 200 per cent, chemical fertilizer 330 per cent, tractors 520 per cent, cotton yarn 85 per cent and chemical fibres 330 per cent. Through our own efforts in these ten years we have completed 1,100 big and medium-sized projects, successfully carried out hydrogen bomb tests and launched man-made earth satellites. In contrast to the economic turmoil and inflation in the capitalist world, we have maintained a balance between our national revenue and expenditure and contracted to external or internal debts. Prices have remained stable, the people's livelihood has steadily improved and socialist construction has flourished. Reactionaries at home and abroad asserted that the Great Proletarian Cultural Revolution would certainly disrupt the development of our national economy, but facts have now given them a strong rebuttal.

Along with the people of other countries, we have won tremendous victories in the struggle against colonialism and imperialism, and in particular against the hegemonism of the superpowers. We have smashed imperialist and social-imperialist encirclement, blockade, aggression and subversion, and have strengthened our unity with the people of all countries, and especially the third world countries. China's seat in the United Nations, of which she had long been illegally deprived, has been restored to her. The number of countries having diplomatic relations with us has increased to nearly 100, and more than 150 countries and regions have economic and trade relations and cultural exchanges with us. Our struggle has won widespread sympathy and support from the people of all countries. We have friends all over the world.

Tempered in the Great Proletarian Cultural Revolution and the movement to criticize Lin Piao and Confucius, our people of all nationalities are more united and our army has grown stronger. Our great motherland is still more consolidated. All our successes are great victories for Marxism-Leninism-Mao Tsetung Thought and for Chairman Mao's revolutionary line.

Fellow Deputies!

The Tenth National Congress of our Party again elucidated the Party's basic line and policies formulated by Chairman Mao for the entire historical period of socialism, and pointed out even more clearly the orientation for continuing the revolution under the dictatorship of the proletariat. Under the leadership of the Party Central Committee headed by Chairman Mao, the people of all our nationalities should unite still more closely, adhere to the Party's basic line and policies, endeavour to fulfill the various fighting tasks set forth by the Party's Tenth Congress, consolidate and enhance the victories of the Great Proletarian Cultural Revolution and strive for new victories in socialist revolution and socialist construction.

Our primary task is to continue to broaden, deepen and persevere in the movement to criticize Lin Piao and Confucius. The struggle between the two classes, the proletariat and the bourgeoisie, between the two roads, the socialist and the capitalist and between the two lines, the Marxist and the revisionist, is long and tortuous and at times even becomes very acute. We must never relax our criticism of Lin Piao and Confucius because of the big successes already achieved in this movement. We should go on deepening the criticism of Lin Piao's revisionist line and the doctrines of Confucius and Mencius, and in line with the principle of making the past serve the present, sum up the historical experience of the struggle between the Confucian and the Legalist schools and of class struggle as a whole, build up a vast Marxist theoretical force in the course of struggle and use Marxism to occupy all spheres in the superstructure. The key to the fulfilment of this task is for the cadres and the masses to study works by Marx, Engels, Lenin and Stalin and by Chairman Mao assiduously in order to arm themselves with the basic theories of Marxism. Through the criticism of Lin Piao and Confucius, we should further advance the revolution in literature and art, in education and in health work, promote struggle-criticism-transformation on various fronts and support all the new things so as the better to keep to the socialist orientation.

Under the leadership of the Party, we should strengthen revolutionary committees at all levels. Leading bodies at all levels should become more conscious of the need to implement Chairman Mao's revolutionary line and should maintain closer ties with the masses. We should make active efforts to train young cadres, women cadres and minority nationality cadres, and make a point of selecting outstanding workers and poor and lower-middle peasants for leading posts. We should have better staff and simpler administration with fewer levels. New and veteran cadres should learn from each other and strengthen their unity, and they should be ready to work at any post, high or low, persist in collective productive labour and wholeheartedly serve the people.

We should strictly distinguish between the two different types of contradictions and handle them correctly, implement the Party's policies conscientiously and ensure that the task of consolidating the dictatorship of the proletariat is fulfilled right through to the grass-roots level. We should rely on the broad masses to deal steady, accurate and hard blows at the handful of class enemies, with the emphasis on accuracy. We should earnestly strive to do well in resolving contradictions among the people with democratic methods in accordance with the principle of unity—criticism and self-criticism—unity, and thus give full play to the masses' enthusiasm for socialism.

The unification of our country, the unity of our people and the unity of our various nationalities—these are the basic guarantees of the sure triumph of our cause. We should strengthen the great unity of the people of all our nationalities. We should wholeheartedly rely on the working class and the poor and lower-middle peasants, unite with the other working people and the many inellectuals and further develop the revolutionary united front which, led by the working class and based on the worker-peasant alliance, includes the patriotic democratic parties, patriotic personages, patriotic overseas Chinese and our compatriots in Hongkong and Macao. We should unit over 95 per cent of the cadres and the masses and unit with all the forces that can be united with in a joint effort to build our great socialist motherland.

Socialist revoltuion is the powerful engine for developing the social productive forces. We must adhere to the principle of grasping revolution, promoting production and other work and preparedness against war, and with revolution in command, work hard to increase production and speed up socialist construction so that our socialist system will have a more solid material foundation.

On Chairman Mao's instructions, it was suggested in the report on the work of the government to the Third National People's Congress that we might envisage the development of our national economy in two stages beginning from the Third Five-Year Plan: The first stage is to build an independent and relatively comprehensive industrial and economic system in 15 years, that is, before 1980; the second stage is to accomplish the comprehensive modernization of agriculture, industry, national defence and science and technology before the end of the century, so that our national economy will be advancing in the front ranks of the world.

We should fulfill or overfulfill the Fourth Five-Year Plan in 1975 in order to reinforce the foundations for completing the first stage before 1980 as envisaged above. In the light of the situation at home and abroad, the next ten years are crucial for accomplishing what has been envisaged for the two stages. In this period we shall not only build an independent and relatively comprehensive industrial and economic system, but march towards the splendid goal set for the second stage. With this objective in mind, the State Council will draw up a long-range ten-year plan, five-year plans and annual plans. The ministries and commissions under the State Council and the local revolutionary committees at all levels down to the industrial and mining enterprises and production teams and other grass-roots units should all arouse the masses to work out their plans through full discussion and strive to attain our splendid goal ahead of time.

In order to keep on expanding our socialist economy, we must persist in the general line of going all out, aiming high and achieving greater, faster, better and more economical results in building socialism and continue to apply the policy of taking agriculture as the foundation and industry as the leading factor and the series of policies of walking on two legs. We should work out the national economic plan in this order of priorities: agriculture, light industry, heavy industry. We should give full play to the initiative of both central and local authorities under the state's unified planning. We should implement the Charter of the Anshan Iron and Steel Company still better and deepen the mass movements—In industry, learn from Taching and In agriculture, learn from Tachai.

While tackling economic tasks, our leading comrades at all levels must pay close attention to the socialist revolution in the realm of the superstructure and keep a firm grasp on class struggle and the struggle between the two lines. Only when we do well in revolution is it possible to do well in production. We should thoroughly criticize revisionism, criticize capitalist tendencies and criticize such erroneous ideas and styles of work as servility to things foreign, the doctrine of trailing behind at a snail's space, and extravagance and waste.

Chairman Mao points out, "Rely mainly on our own efforts while making external assistance subsidiary, break down blind faith, go in for industry, agriculture and technical and cultural revolutions independently, do away with slavishness, bury dogmatism, learn from the good experience of other countries conscientiously and be sure to study their bad experience too, so as to draw lessons from it. This is our line." This line has enabled us to break the imperialist blockade and withstand social-imperialist pressure, and the progress of our economy has been sound and vigorous all along, regardless of economic fluctuations and crises in the capitalist world. We must always adhere to this line.

Fellow Deputies!

The present international situation is still characterized by great disorder under heaven, a disorder which is growing greater and greater. The capitalist world is facing the most serious economic crisis since the war, and all the basic contradictions in the world are sharpening. On the one hand, the trend of revolution by the people of the world is actively developing; countries want independence, nations want liberation, and the people want revolution—this has become an irresistible historical current. On the other hand, the contention for world hegemony between the two superpowers, the United States and the Soviet Union, is becoming more and more intense. Their contention has extended to every corner of the world, the focus of their contention being Europe. Soviet social-imperialism "makes a feint to the east while attacking in the west." The two superpowers, the United States and the Soviet Union, are the biggest international oppressors and exploiters today, and they are the source of a new world war. Their fierce contention is bound to lead to world war some day. The people of all countries must get prepared. Detente and peace are being talked about everywhere in the world; it is precisely this that shows there is no detente, let alone lasting peace, in this world. At present, the factors for both revolution and war are increasing. Whether war gives rise to revolution or revolution prevents war, in either case the international situation will develop in a direction favourable to the people and the future of the world will be bright.

We should continue to implement Chairman Mao's revolutionary line in foreign affairs, always keep the people in mind, place our hopes on them and do our external work better. We should uphold proletarian internationalism and strengthen our unity with the socialist countries and all the oppressed people and oppressed nations of the world, with each supporting the other. We should ally ourselves with all the forces in the world that can be allied with to combat colonialism, imperialism and above all superpower hegemonism. We are ready to establish or develop relations with all countries on the basis of the Five Principles of Peaceful Coexistence.

The third world is the main force in combating colonialism, imperialism and hegemonism. China is a developing socialist country belonging to the third world. We should enhance our unity with the countries and people of Asia, Africa and Latin America and resolutely support them in their struggle to win or safeguard national independence, defend their state sovereignty, protect their national resources and develop their national economy. We firmly support the just struggles of the people of Korea, Viet Nam, Cambodia, Laos, Palestine and the Arab countries as well as countries in southern Africa. We support the countries and people of the second world in their struggle against superpower control, threats and bullying. We support the efforts of West European countries to get united in this struggle. We are ready to work together with the Japanese Government and people to promote friendly and good-neighbourly relations between the two countries on the basis of the Sino-Japanese Joint Statement.

There exist fundamental differences between China and the United States. Owing to the joint efforts of both sides the relations between the two countries have improved to some extent in the last three years, and contacts between the two peoples have developed. The relations between the two countries will continue to improve so long as the principles of the Sino-American Shanghai Communique are carried out in earnest.

The Soviet leading clique have betrayed Marxism-Leninism, and our debate with them on matters of principle will go on for a long time. However, we have always held that this debate should not obstruct the maintenance of normal state relations between China and the Soviet Union. The Soviet leadership have taken a series of steps to worsen the relations between the two countries, conducted subversive activities against our country and even provoked armed conflicts on the border. In violation of the understanding reached between the Premiers of China and the Soviet Union as early as 1969, they refuse to sign the agreement on the maintenance of the status quo on the border, the prevention of armed conflicts and the disengagement of the armed forces of the two sides in the disputed areas on the border, an agreement which includes the non-use of force against each other and mutual non-aggression. Hence the negotiations on the Sino-Soviet boundary question have so far yielded no results. They even deny the existence of the disputed areas on the Sino-Soviet border, and they even refuse to do anything about such matters as the disengagement of the armed forces of the two sides in the disputed areas on the border and the prevention of armed conflicts instead they talk profusely about empty treaties on the non-use of force against each other and mutual non-aggression. So what can their real intention be if not to deceive the Soviet people and world public opinion? We wish to advise the Soviet leadership to sit down and negotiate honestly, do something to solve a bit of the problem and stop playing such deceitful tricks.

Chairman Mao teaches us, "Dig tunnels deep, store grain everywhere, and never seek hegemony." "Be prepared against war, be prepared against natural disasters, and do everything for the people." We should maintain vigilance, strengthen our defence and be prepared against war. The heroic People's Liberation Army shoulders the glorious task of defending the motherland. The whole army should resolutely implement Chairman Mao's line for army building to strengthen the army and enhance preparedness against war. We should build the people's militia conscientiously and well. Together with the people of all our nationalities, the People's Liberation Army and the masses of the people's militia should be ready at all times to wipe out any enemy that dares intrude.

We are determined to liberate Taiwan! Fellow countrymen in Taiwan and people of the whole country, unite and work together to achieve the noble aim of liberating Taiwan and unifying the motherland!

Fellow Deputies!

In the excellent situation prevailing at home and abroad, we should first of all run China's affairs well and strive to make a greater contribution to humanity.

We must bear firmly in mind Chairman Mao's teachings and grasp major issues, grasp the line, and adhere to these fundamental principles, "Practise Marxism, and not revisionism; unite, and don't split; be open and aboveboard, and don't intrigue and conspire."

We must resolutely support the centralized leadership of the Party. Of the seven sectors—industry, agriculture, commerce, culture and education, the Army, the government and the Party—it is the Party that exercises overall leadership. We must put all fields of work under the unified leadership of the Party committees at various levels.

We must carry forward the glorious tradition of observing discipline, conscientiously practise democratic centralism, and, on the basis of Chairman Mao's revolutionary line, achieve unity in thinking, policy, plan, command and action.

We must persist in the mass line: From the masses, to the masses; we must have unshakable faith in the vast majority of the masses and firmly rely on them. Both in revolution and in construction, we should boldly arouse the people and unfold vigorous mass movements.

We must work hard, build the country and run all undertakings with diligence and thrift. We should maintain the same vigour, the same revolutionary enthusiasm and the same daring death-defying spirit we displayed in the years of revolutionary war, and carry on our revolutionary work to the end.

We must uphold proletarian internationalism, and get rid of great-power chauvinism resolutely, thoroughly, wholly and completely. We will never seek hegemony; we will never be a superpower; we will always stand with the oppressed people and oppressed nations throughout the world.

Under the leadership of the Central Committee of the Party headed by Chairman Mao, the Chinese people have worked energetically, surmounted all difficulties and hazards, and turned a poverty-stricken and backward country into a socialist one with the beginnings of prosperity in only twenty years and more. We can certainly build China into a powerful modern socialist country in another twenty years and more before the end of the century. We should continue to work hard, carry forward our achievements and overcome our shortcomings, be modest and prudent, guard against arrogance and rashness, and continue our triumphant advance. Under the guidance of Chairman Mao's revolutionary line, let us unite to win still greater victories!

APPENDIX F

China's population by provinces (in millions)

Provinces	Source
Anhwei : 45	September 19, 1976—Provincial Broadcast (PB)
Chekiang : 35	September 29, 1976—PB
Fukien : more than 20	April 15, 1976—PB
Heilungkiang : 32	September 11, 1976—Peoples Daily (PD)
Honan : 60	September 20, 1976—PB
Hopeh : more than 40	June 6, 1975—Peking Review
Hunan : 40	September 17, 1976—PB
Hupeh : 40	September 17, 1976—PB
Inner Mongolia : 8.6 (.44 Mongols)	October 6, 1976—Asian Wall Street Journal. Told Schlesinger group by Chinese officials.
Kansu : 18	September 12, 1976—PD
Kiangsi : 28	September 19, 1976—PB
Kiangsu : 55	September 20, 1976—PD
Kirin : 23	September 19, 1976—PB
Kwangsi : 31	April 13, 1976—PB
Kwangtung : 53.5	Derived from a July 16, 1976 PD article stating that 26% of the people in Kwantung, 13,910,-000 swim.
Kweichow : 24	September 29, 1976—PB
Liaoning : 33	September 11, 1976—PB
Ninghsia : more than 3	April 9, 1976—NCNA Domestic Service
Peking : 8	September 10, 1976—PD
Shanghai : 10	September 18, 1976—City Broadcast
Shansi : 23	September 20, 1976—PD
Shantung : 68	September 20, 1976—PD
Shensi : 26	September 30, 1976—PB
Sinkiang : 11 (41.4% Han)	October 6, 1976—Asian Wall Street Journal
Szechuan : 80	September 20, 1976—PB
Tibet : 1.82 (.12 Han)	October 6, 1976—Asian Wall Street Journal
Tientsin : 7	September 11, 1976—PD
Tsinghai : more than 3	September 20, 1976—PD
Yunnan : 28	September 19, 1976—PB

Total population____ 854.92

Source : U.S. Consulate General, Hong Kong.

INDEX

159